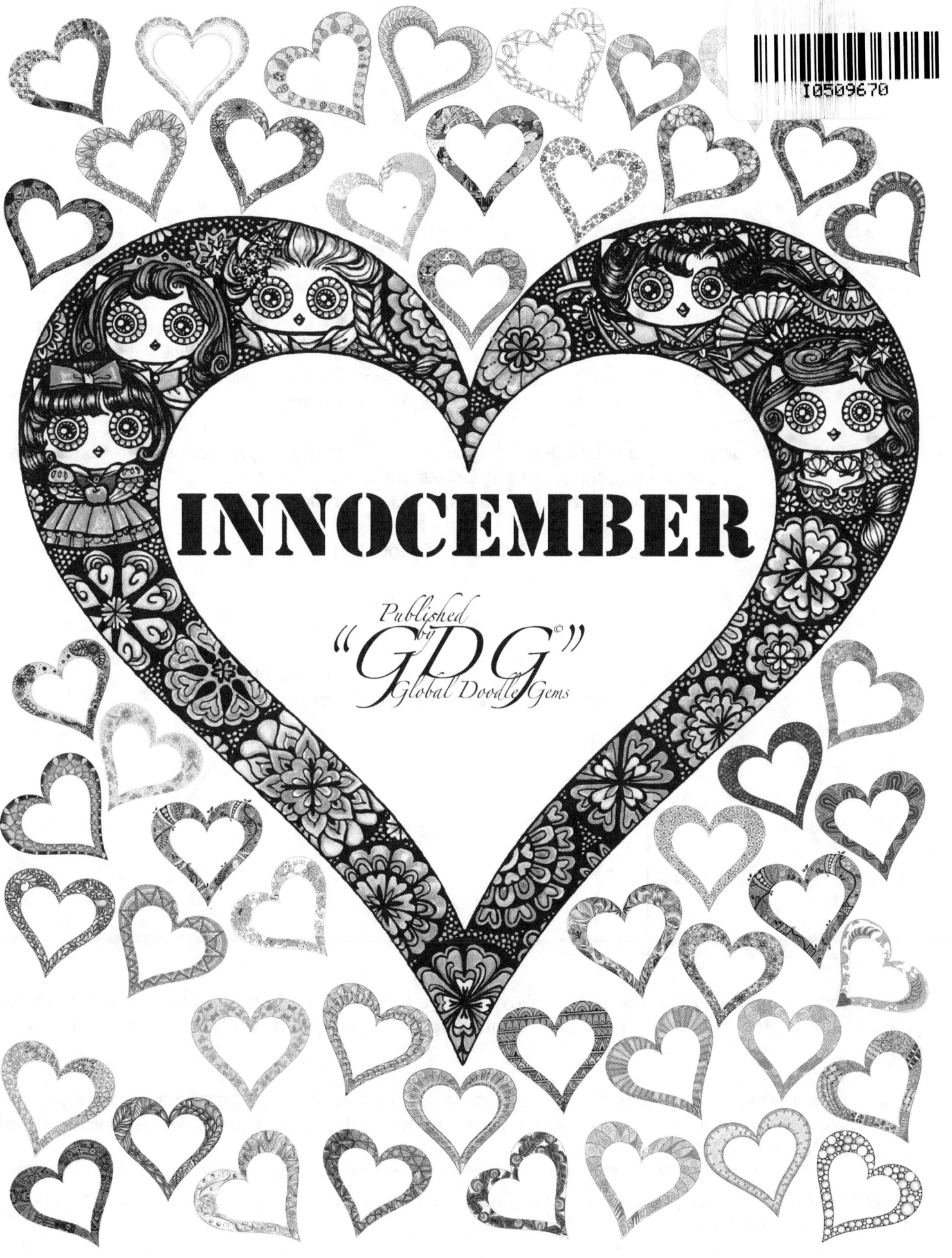

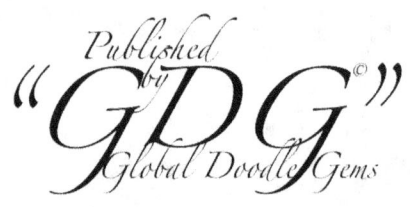

Share your colored versions with us ! We love seeing your results and hearing from you we are social !

The Official FB book page, stay on top of what we have in the works !
www.facebook.com/globaldoodlegems

The Community group, share your colored pages, meet the artists, enjoy exclusive freebies, take part in community Charity books and so much more......
www.facebook.com/groups/globaldoodlegems/

Follow us on Twitter.... @GlobalDoodlegem

We are on Instagram too
@globaldoodlegems for instagram

...and if you are not social like that we have a blog
globaldoodlegems.wordpress.com

Copyright © 2015 Global Doodle Gems

All rights are reserved by Global Doodle Gems.

Duplication of pages for personal use are allowed. You are invited to color the pages then scan/post your coloured versions to social networks, mentioning the book title and author/artist (Global Doodle Gems).

All artwork and images are protected by copyright laws. This book or any portion thereof may not, otherwise, be reproduced and/or distributed or transmitted without the express written permission of the artist/publisher of Global Doodle Gems.

All of us from the Global Doodle Gems wish you a colortastic time and look forward to seeing your wonderful color results online !

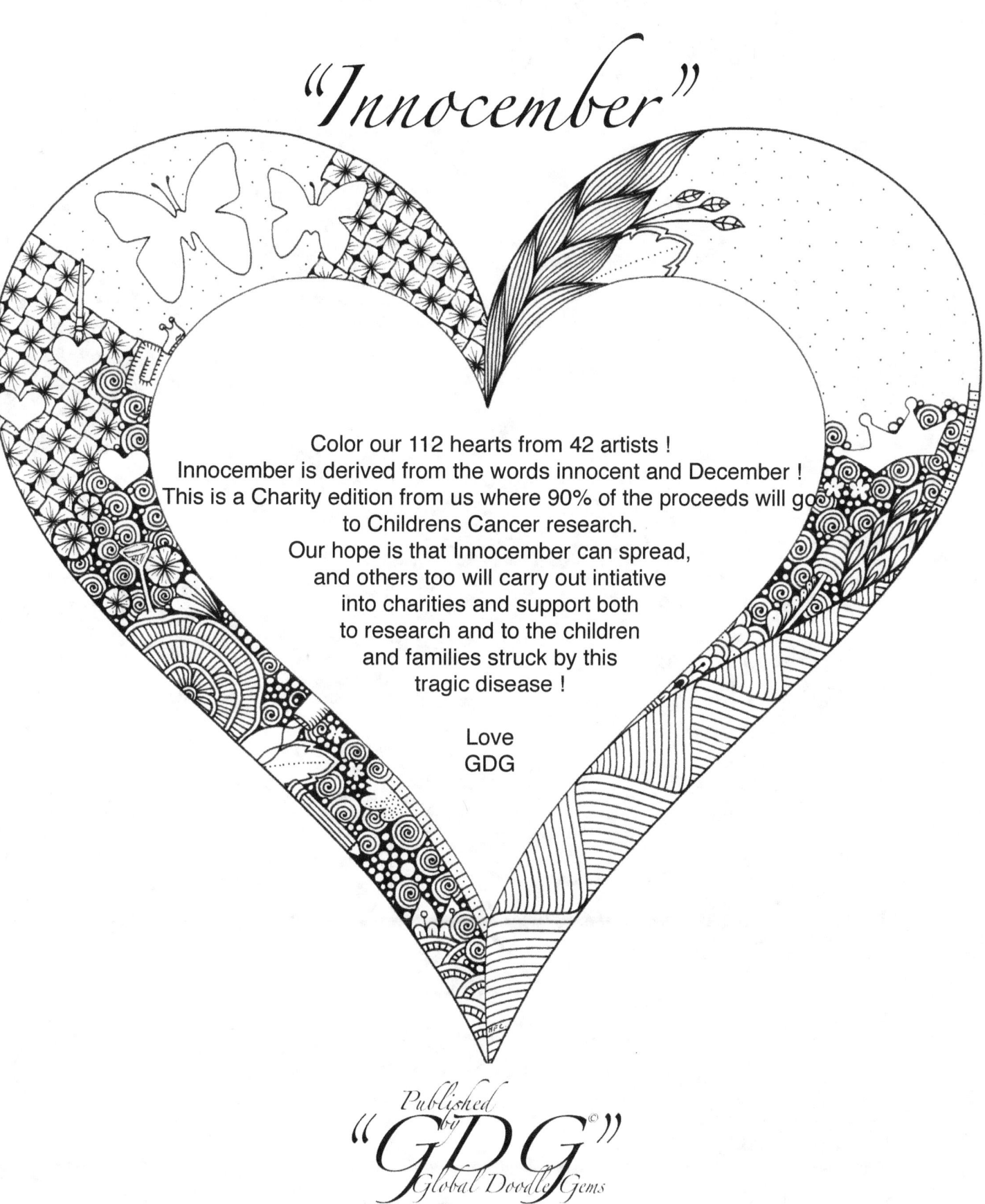

Contributing Artist
Adriana Graciela Volpe
Argentina

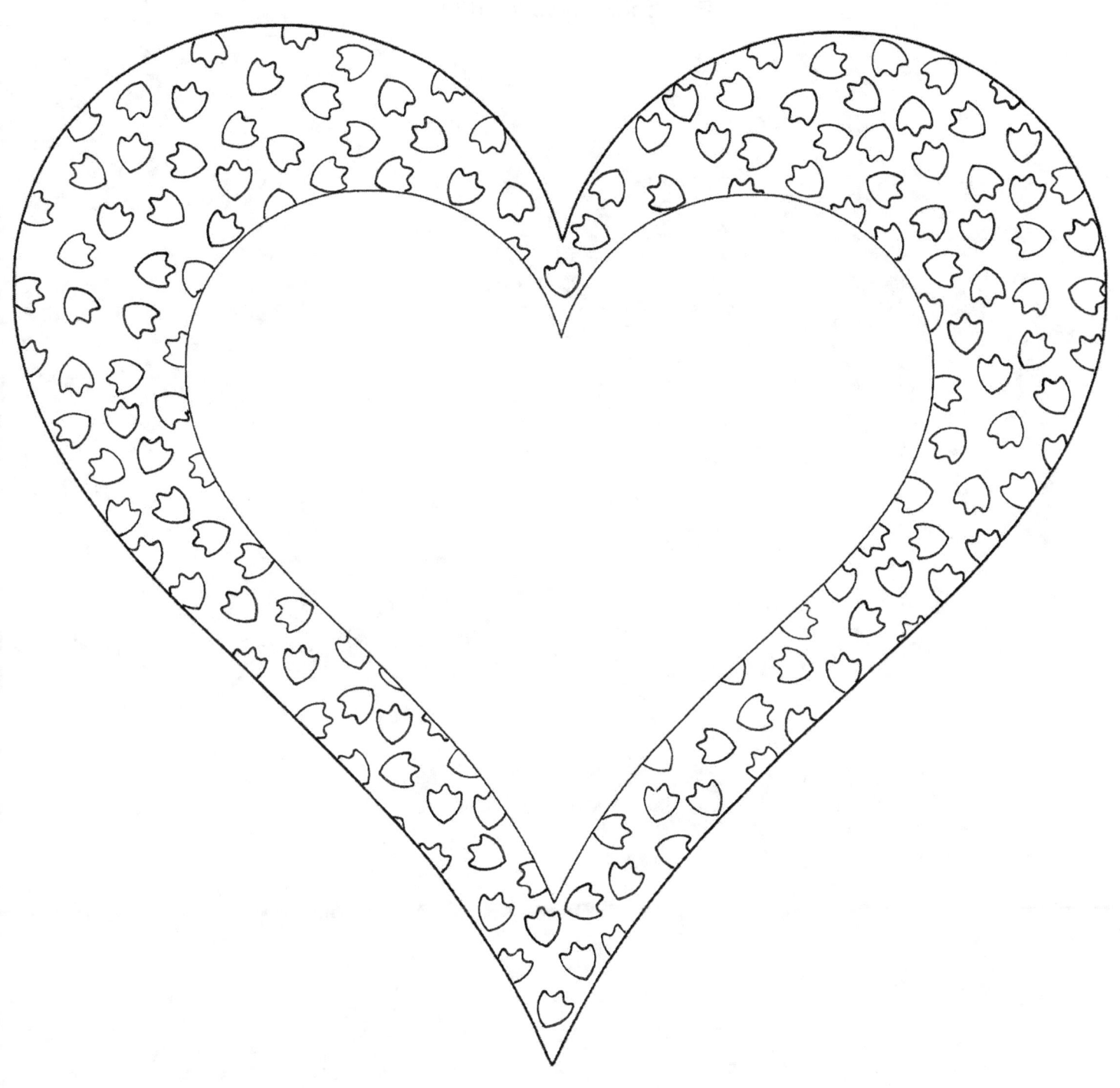

Contributing Artist
Alfred E. Villanueva
Philippines
Facebook : viworksart2015

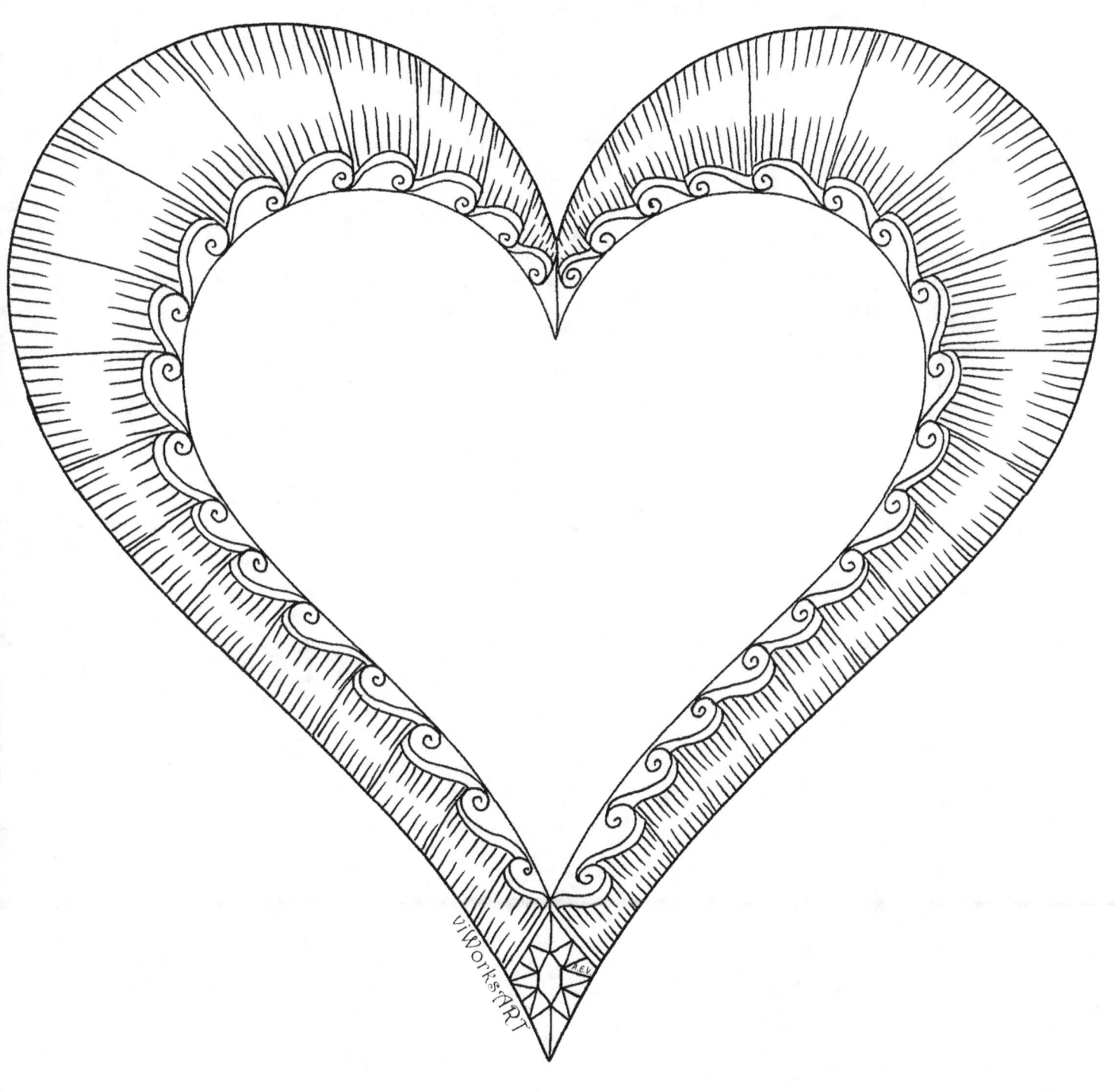

Contributing Artist
Alfred E. Villanueva
Philippines
Facebook : viworksart2015

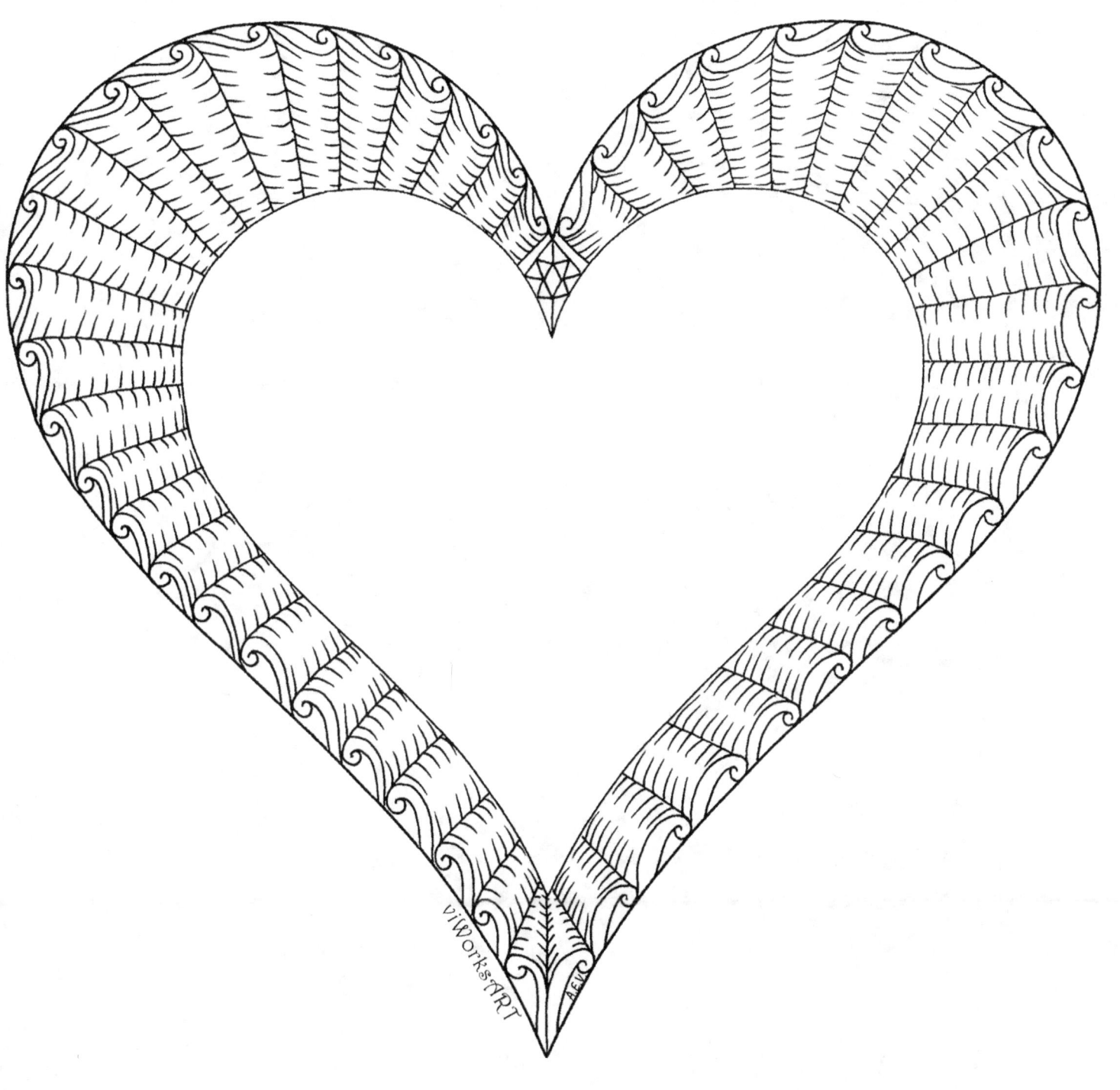

Contributing Artist
Alfred E. Villanueva
Philippines
Facebook : viworksart2015

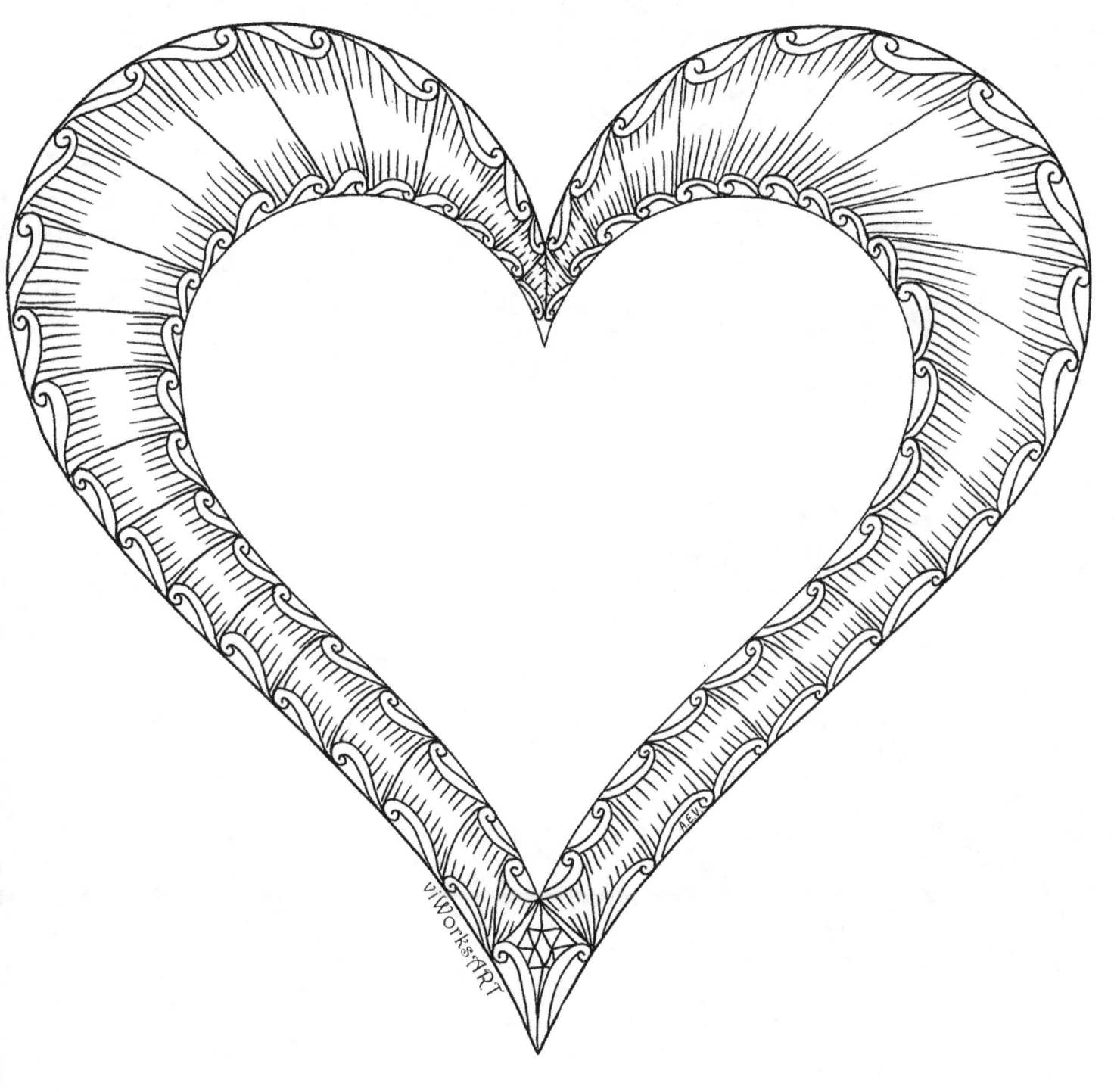

Contributing Artist
Alfred E. Villanueva
Philippines
Facebook : viworksart2015

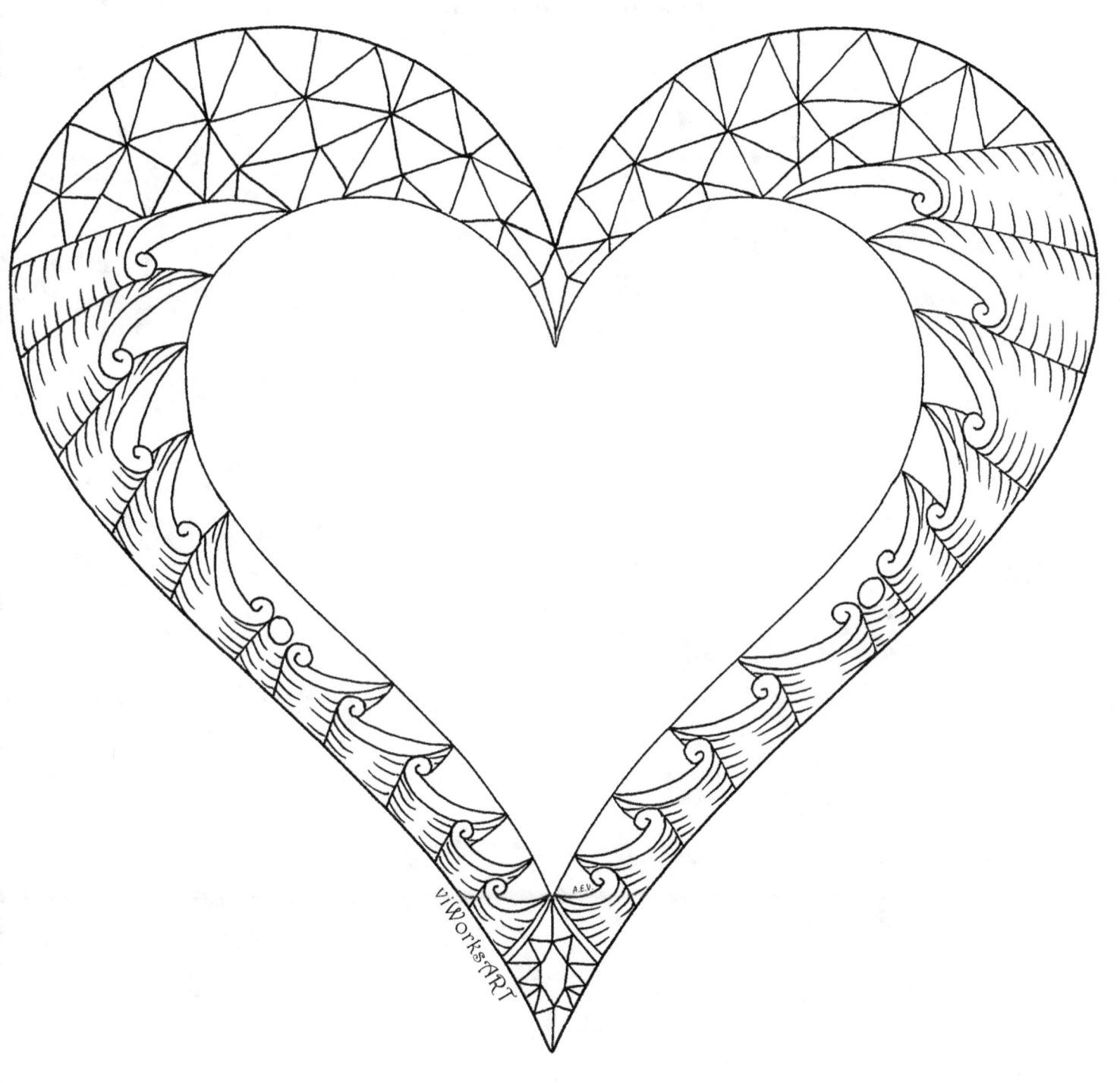

Contributing Artist
Alfred E. Villanueva
Philippines
Facebook : viworksart2015

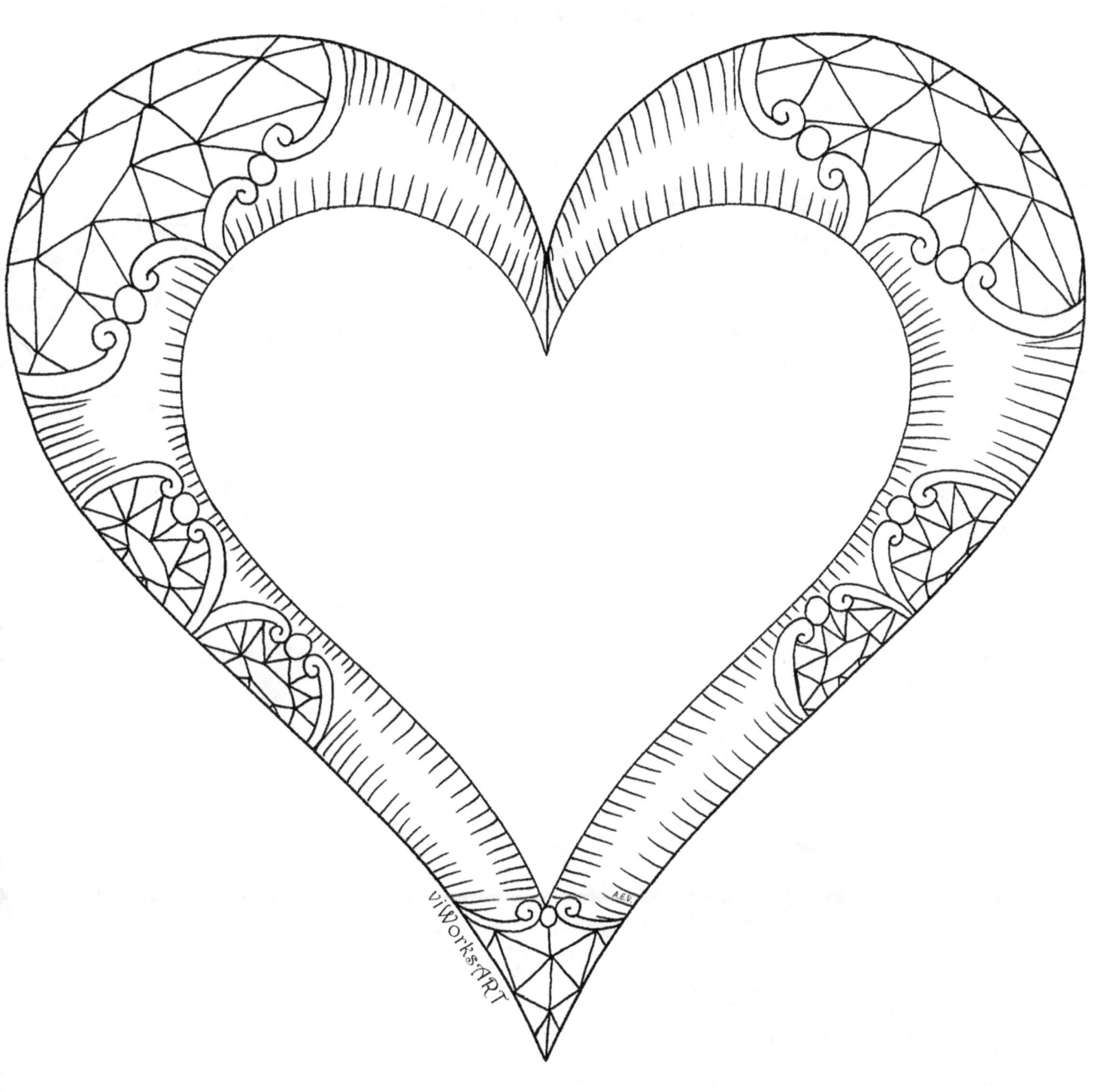

Contributing Artist
Alfred E. Villanueva
Philippines
Facebook : viworksart2015

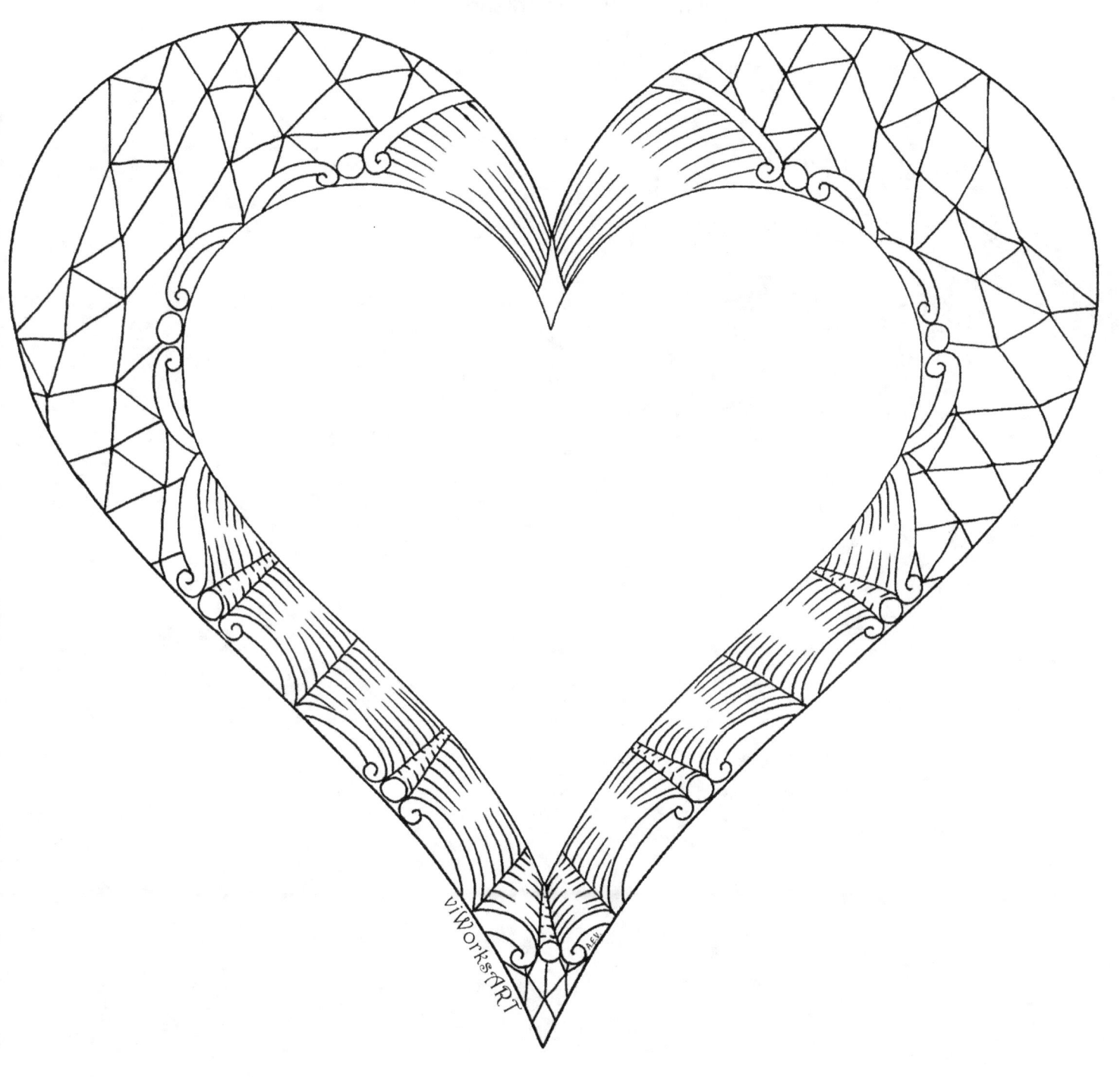

Contributing Artist
Alfred E. Villanueva
Philippines
Facebook : viworksart2015

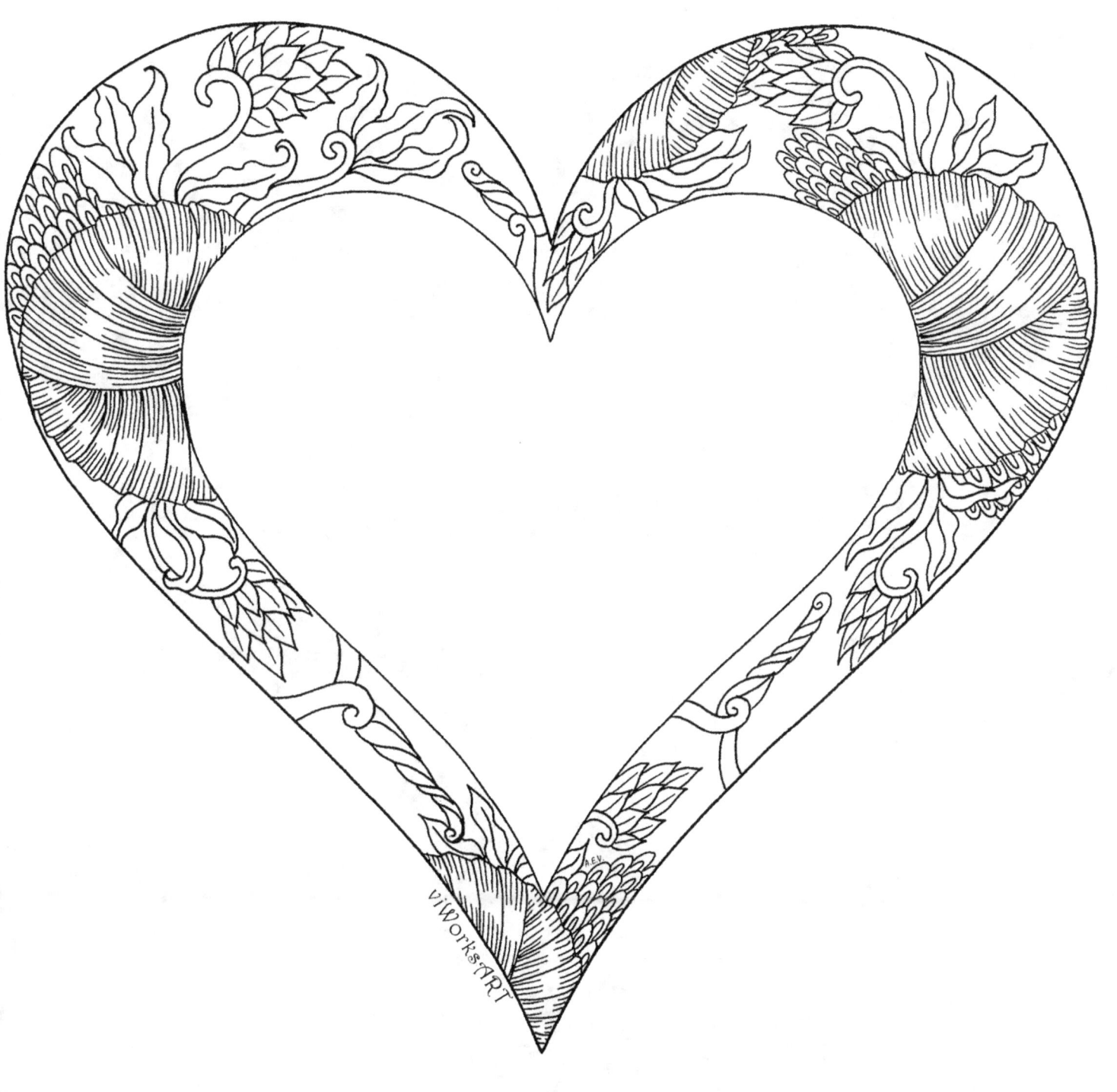

Contributing Artist
Alfred E. Villanueva
Philippines
Facebook : viworksart2015

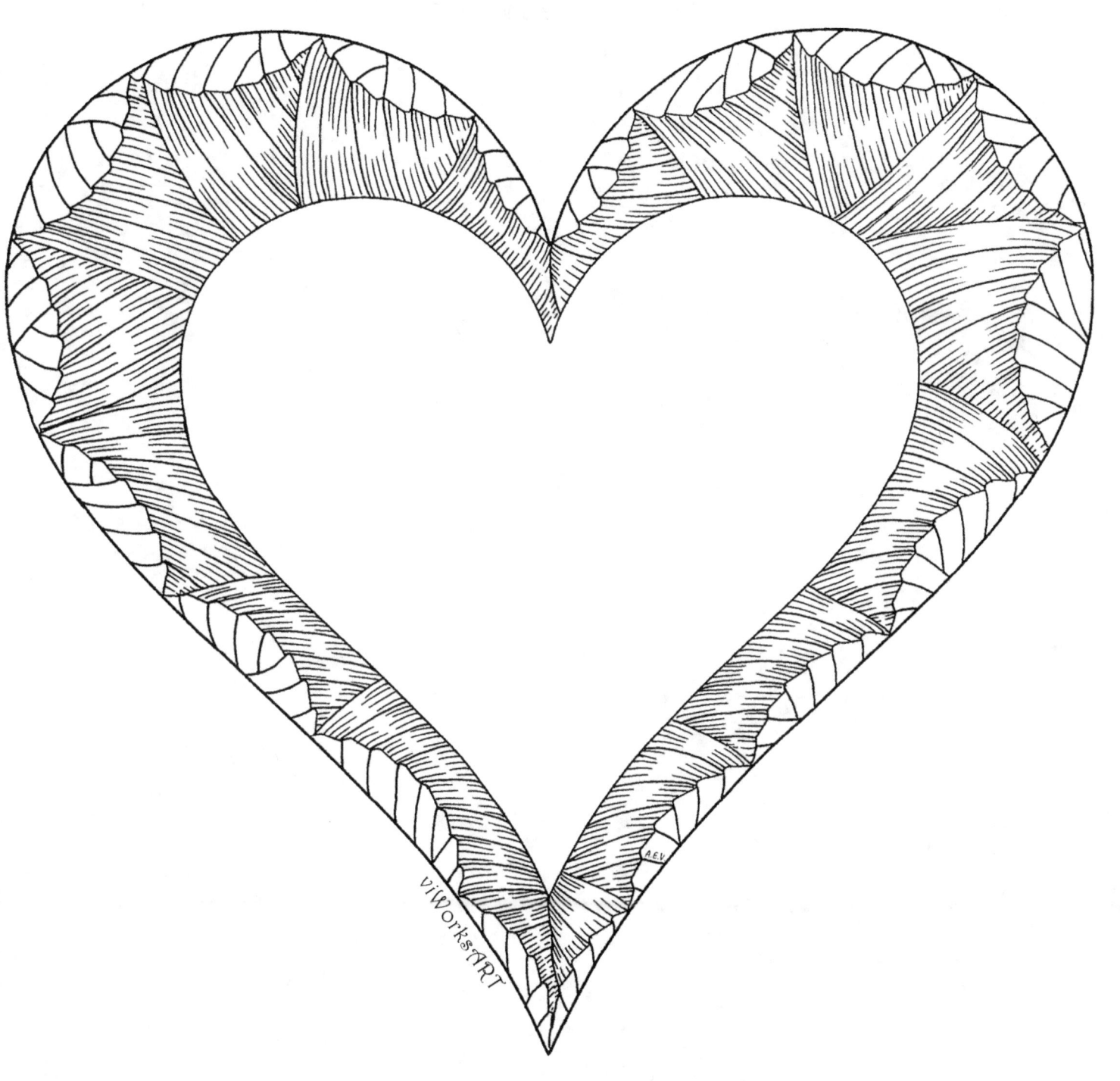

Contributing Artist
Alfred E. Villanueva
Philippines
Facebook : viworksart2015

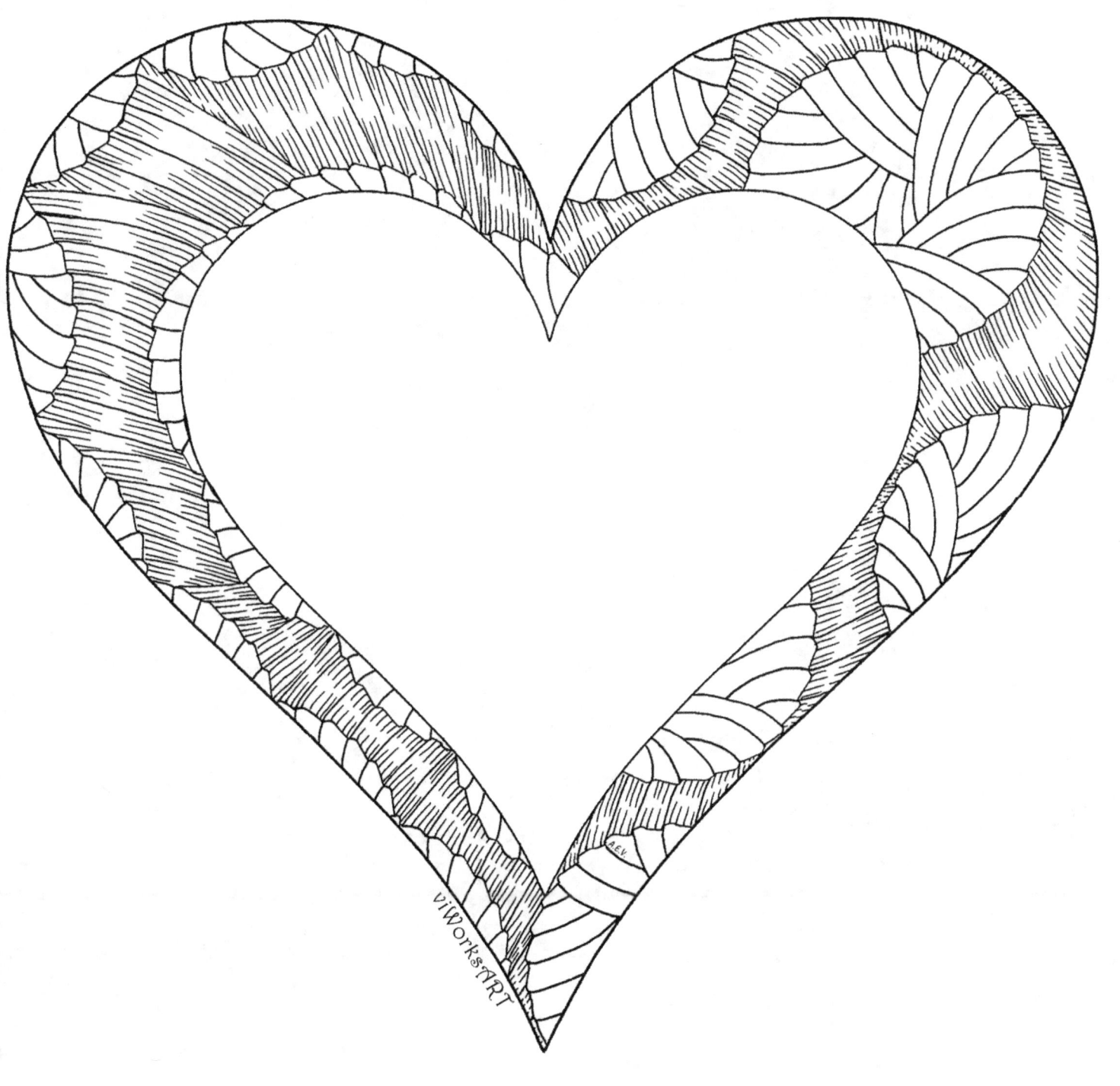

Contributing Artist
Alfred E. Villanueva
Philippines
Facebook : viworksart2015

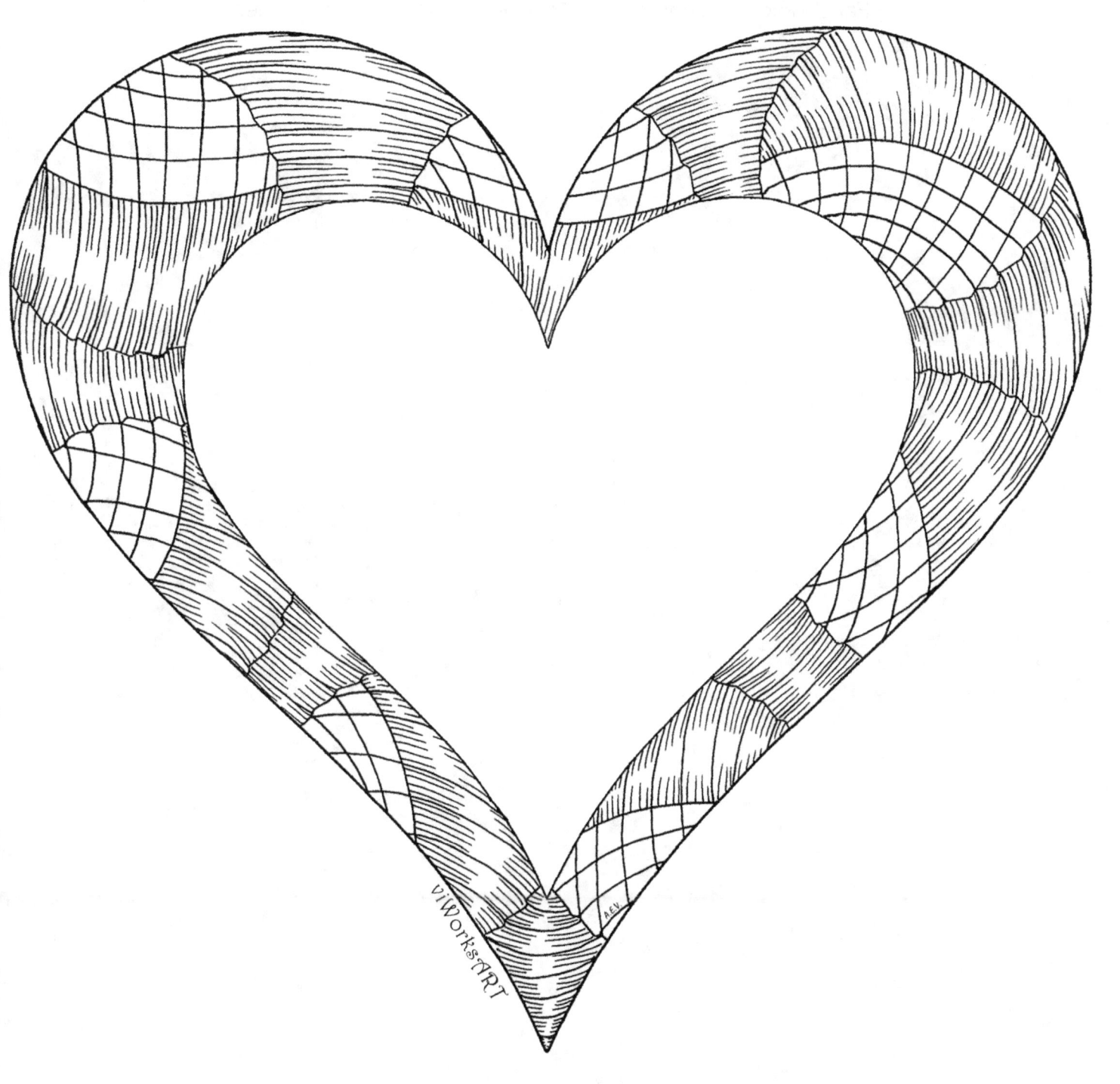

Contributing Artist
Amandine Cyril M.L
France

Facebook : Amandine-Cyril-ML-Mes-dessins-et-coloriages

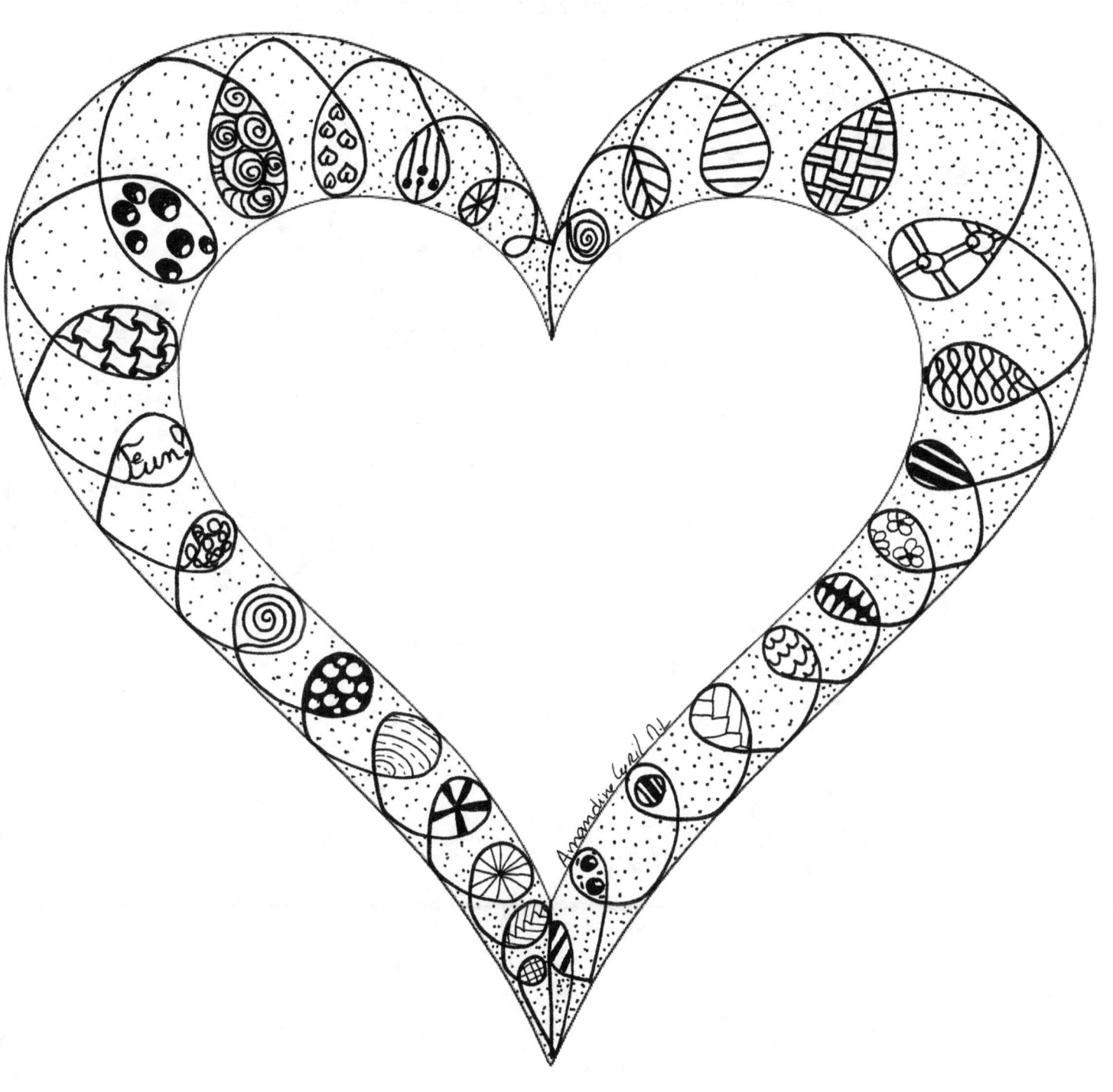

Contributing Artist
Amandine Cyril M.L
France

Facebook : Amandine-Cyril-ML-Mes-dessins-et-coloriages

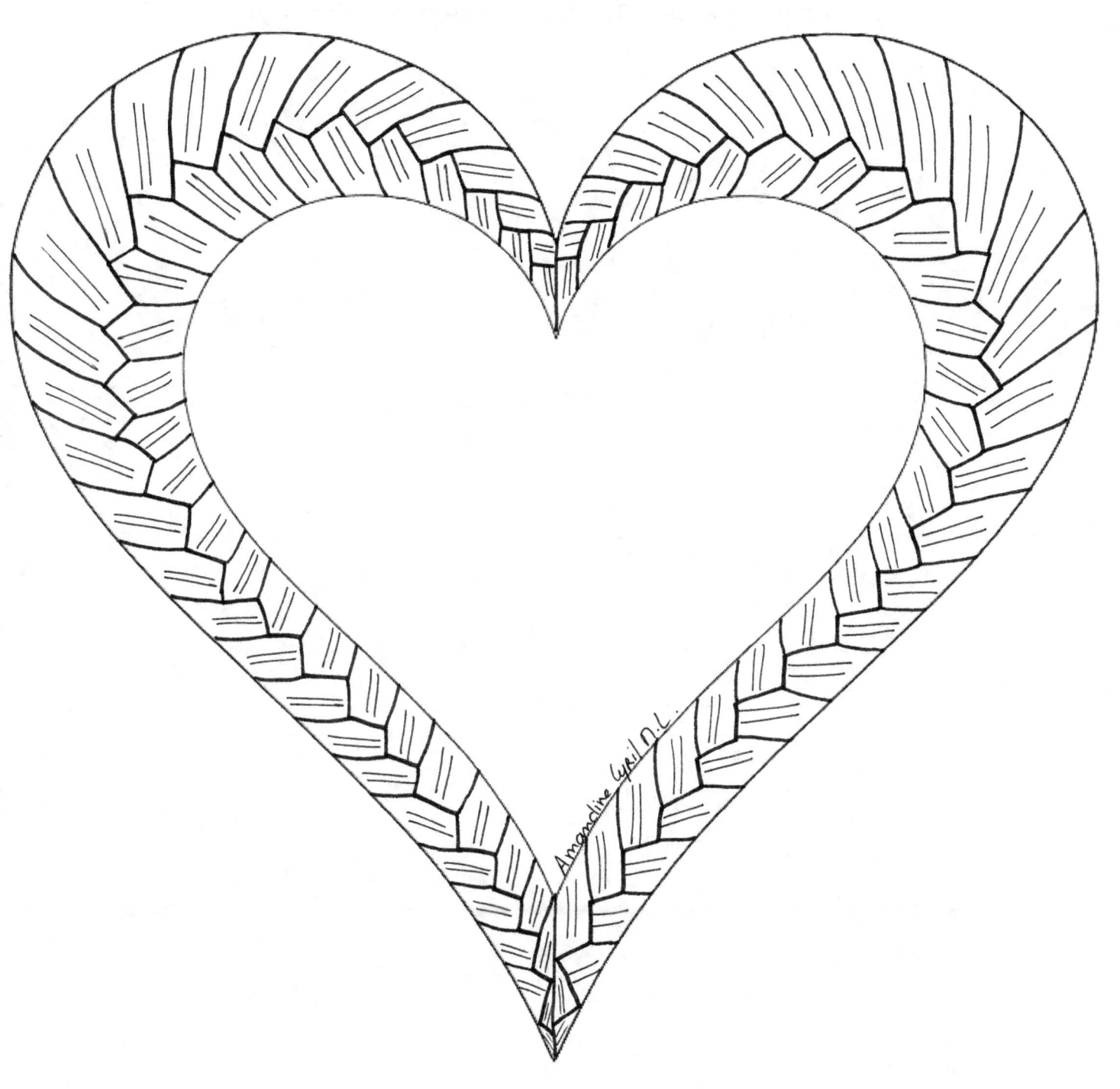

Contributing Artist
Amandine Cyril M.L
France

Facebook : Amandine-Cyril-ML-Mes-dessins-et-coloriages

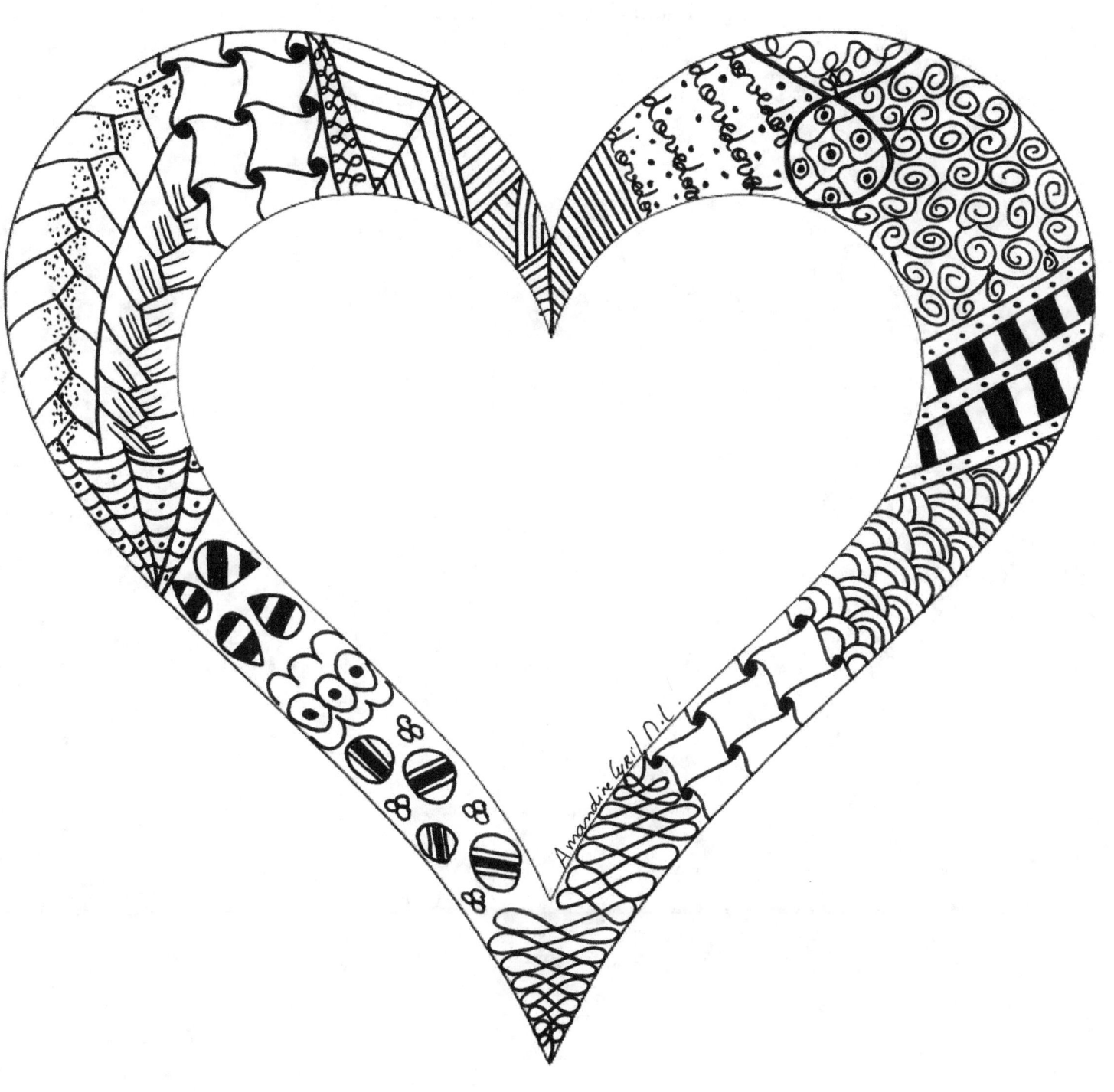

Contributing Artist
Audrey Sagh
Saskatoon, Saskatchewan Canada

Facebook : AMS-Artwork

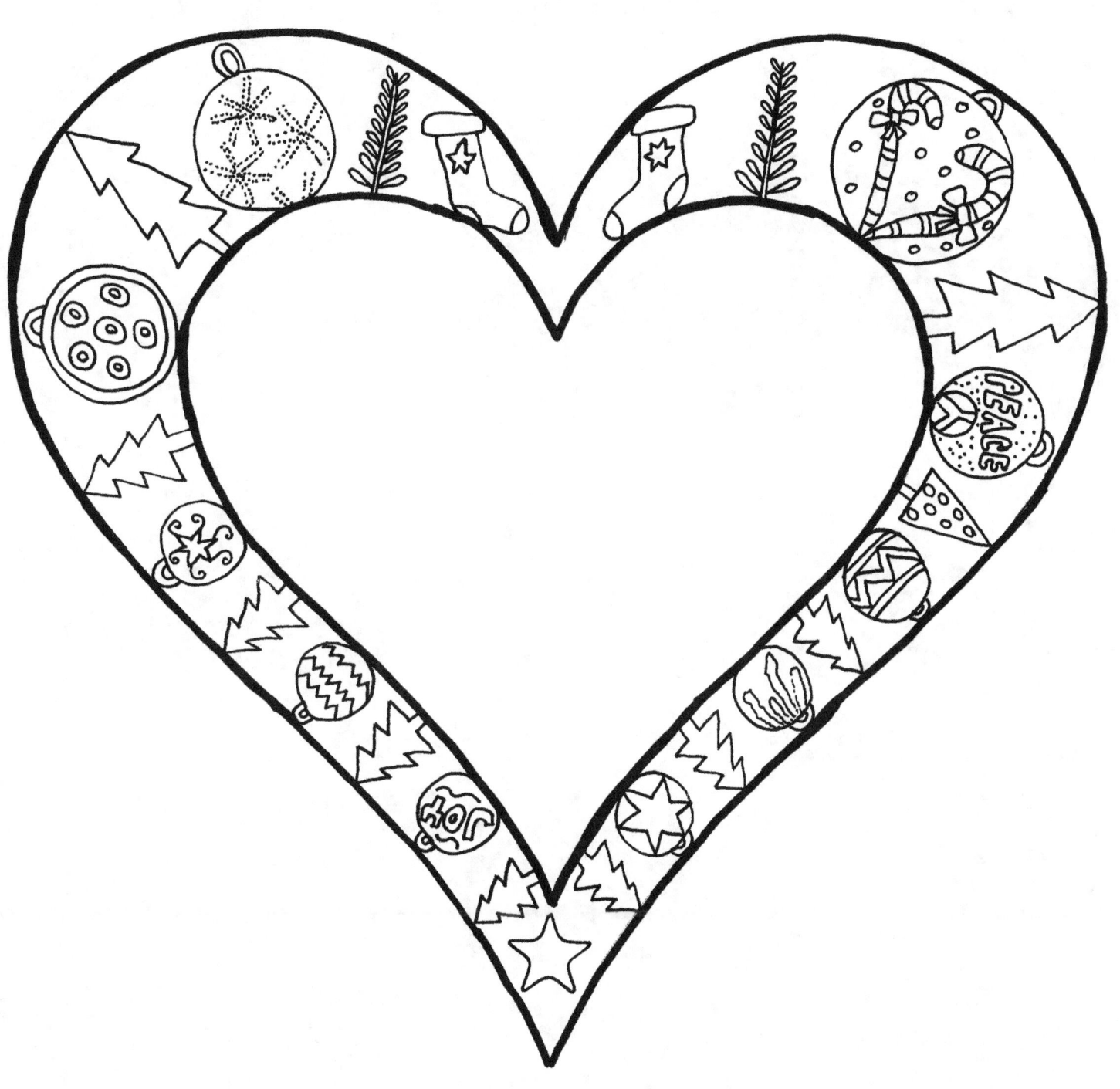

Contributing Artist
Audrey Sagh
Saskatoon, Saskatchewan Canada

Facebook : AMS-Artwork

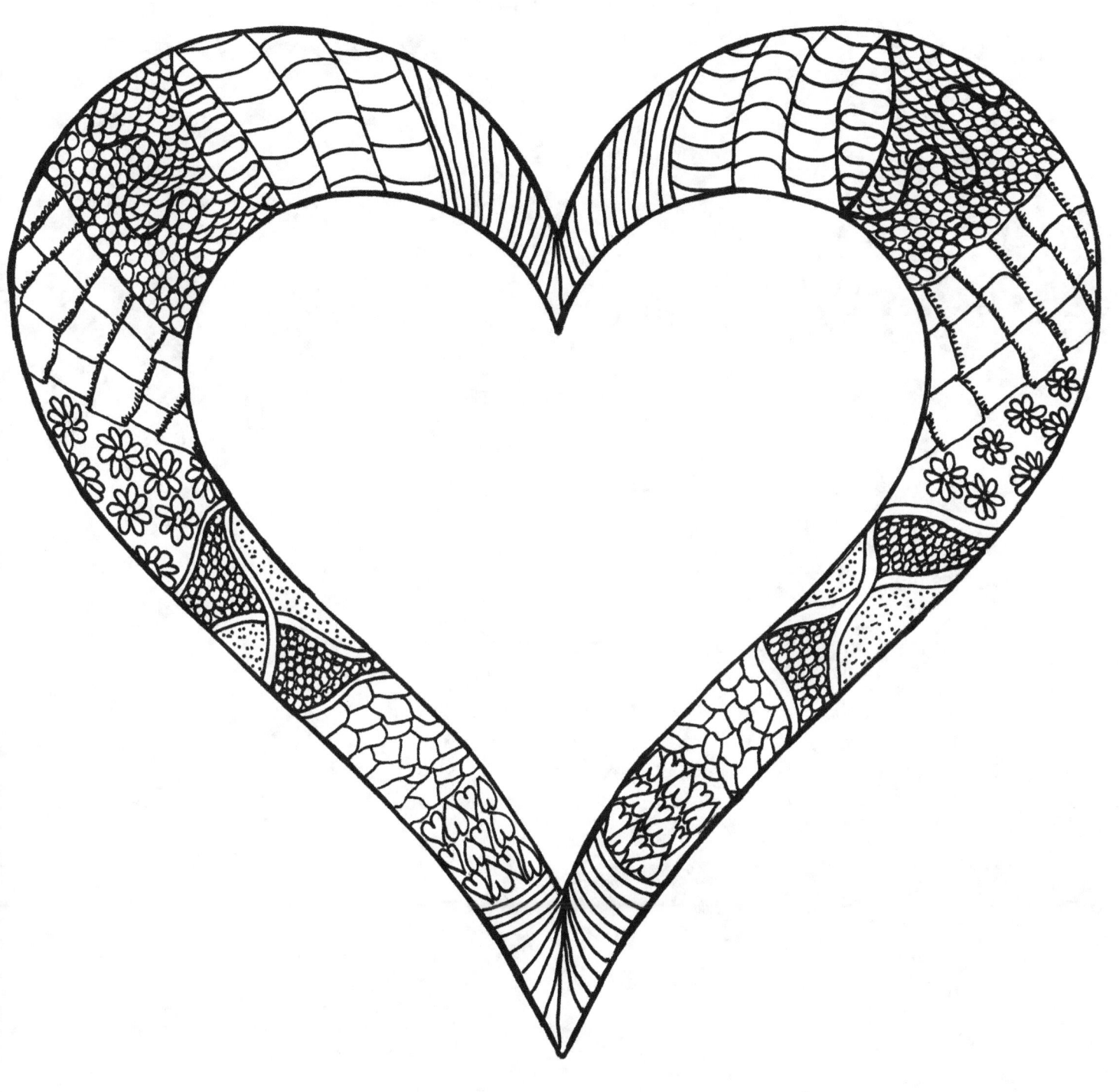

Contributing Artist
Audrey Sagh
Saskatoon, Saskatchewan Canada

Facebook : AMS-Artwork

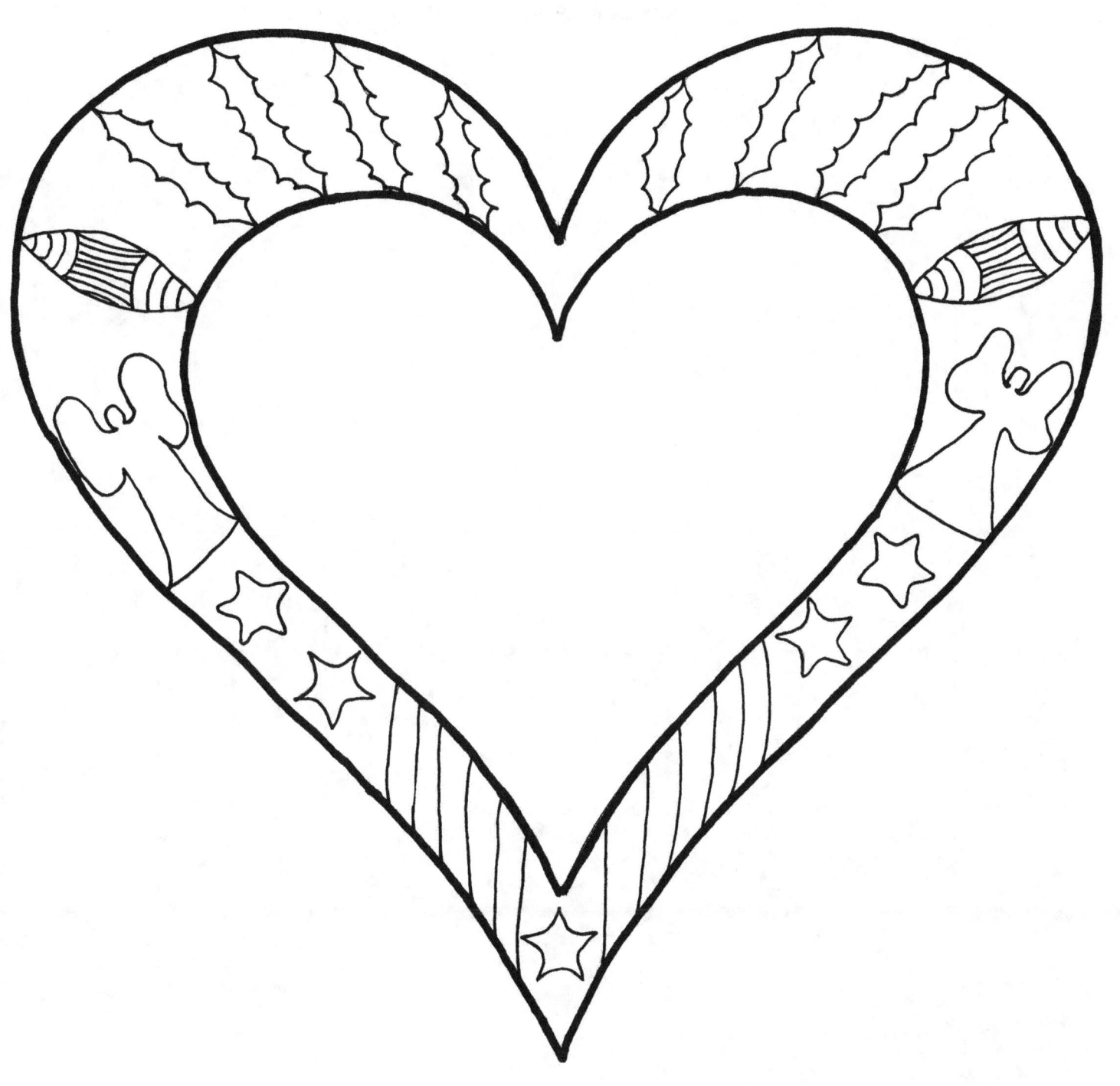

Contributing Artist
Audrey Sagh
Saskatoon, Saskatchewan Canada

Facebook : AMS-Artwork

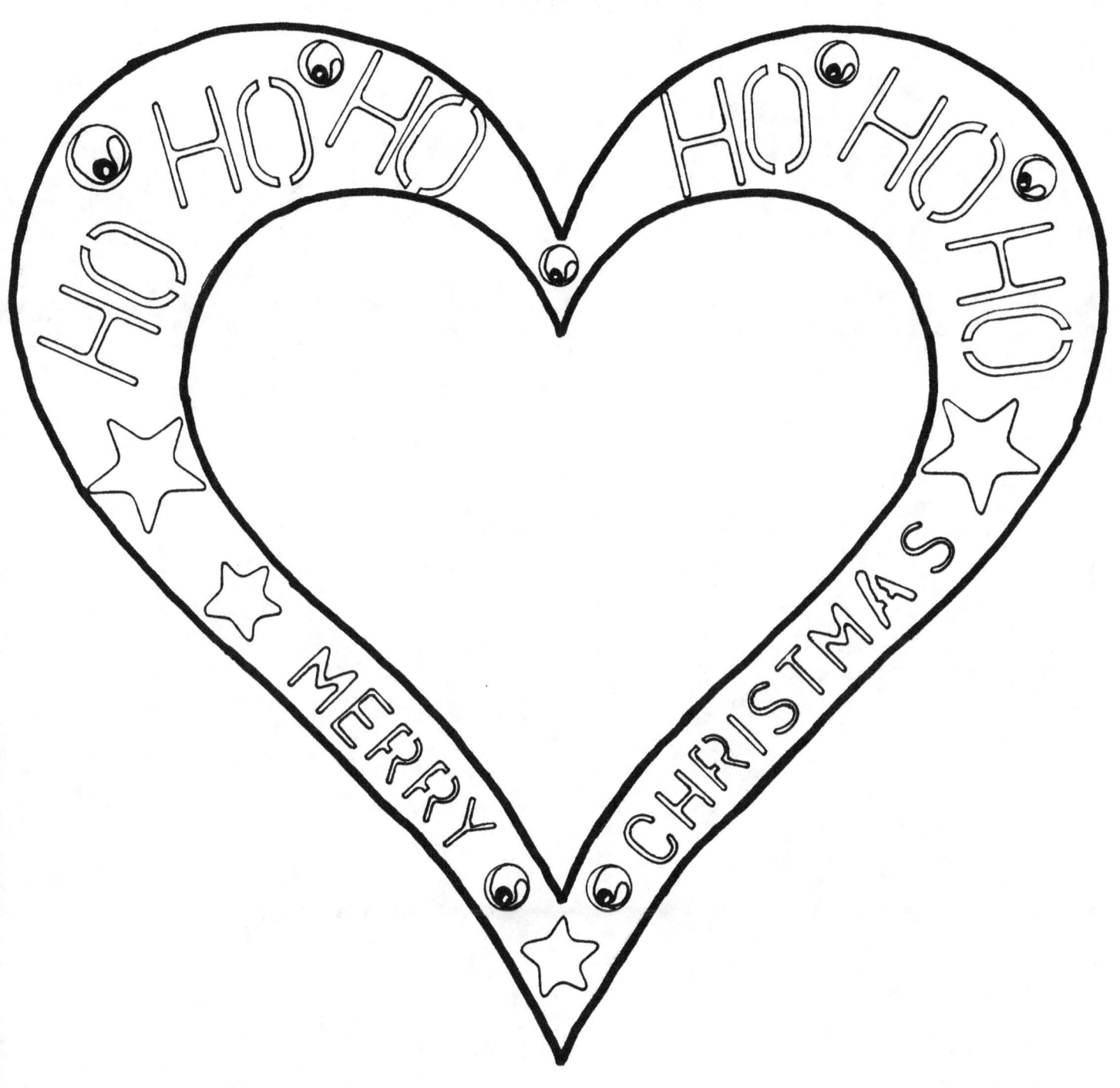

Contributing Artist
Audrey Sagh
Saskatoon, Saskatchewan Canada

Facebook : AMS-Artwork

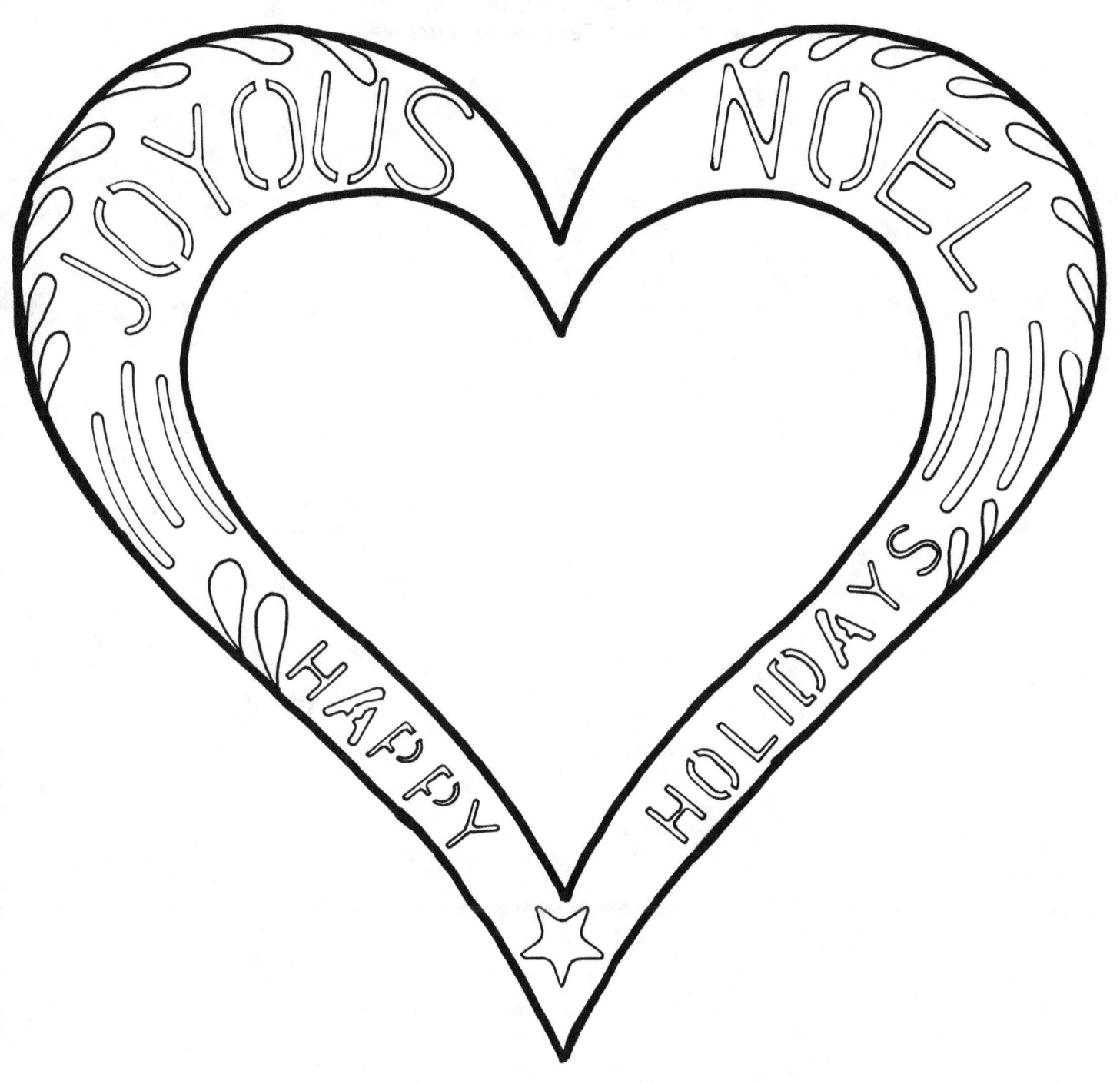

Contributing Artist
Céline Créacolor
France

Facebook : Le-monde-de-Créacolo
Website : www.mon-atelier-des-couleurs.webnode.fr

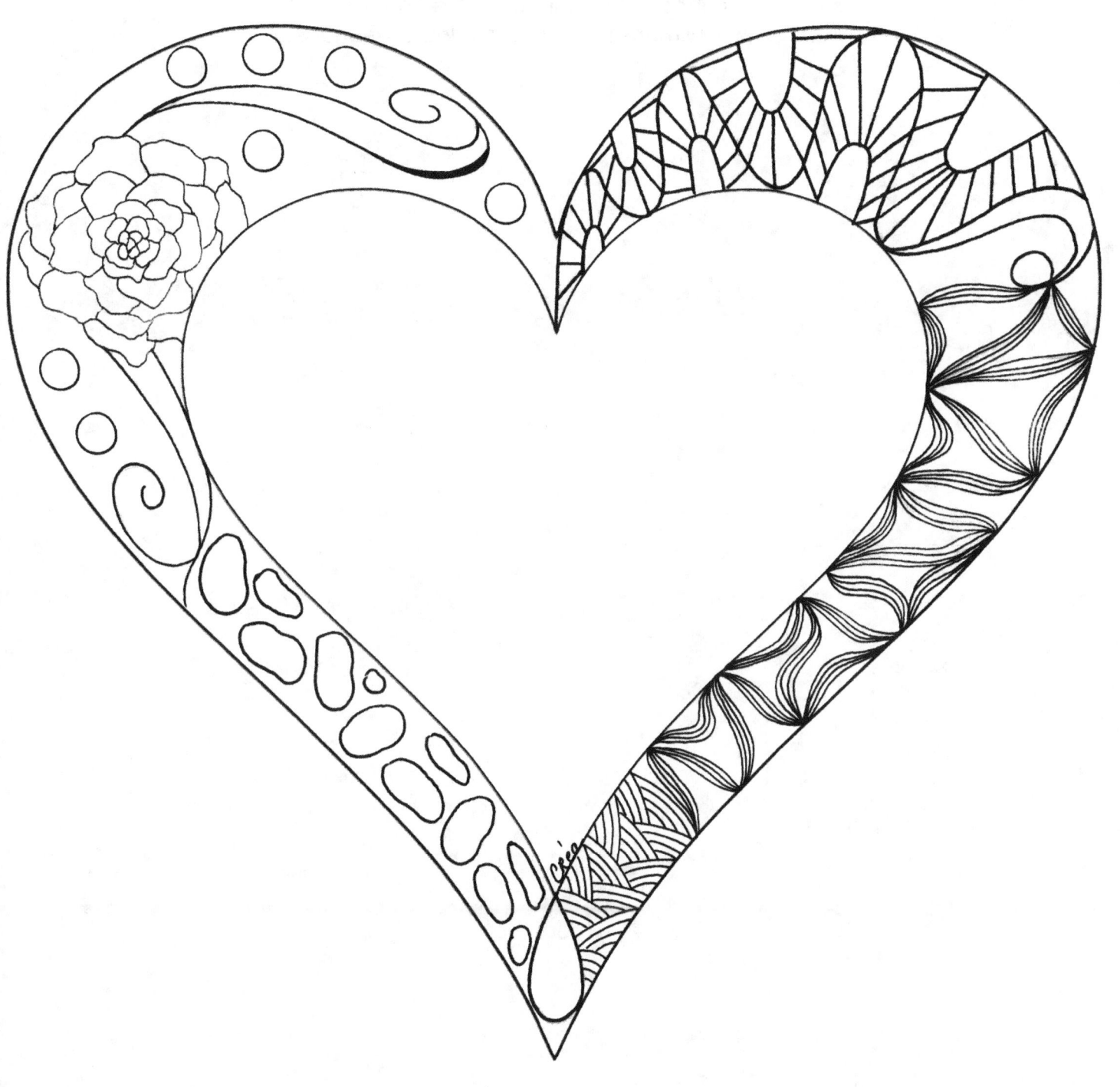

Contributing Artist
Céline Créacolor
France

Facebook : Le-monde-de-Créacolo
Website : www.mon-atelier-des-couleurs.webnode.fr

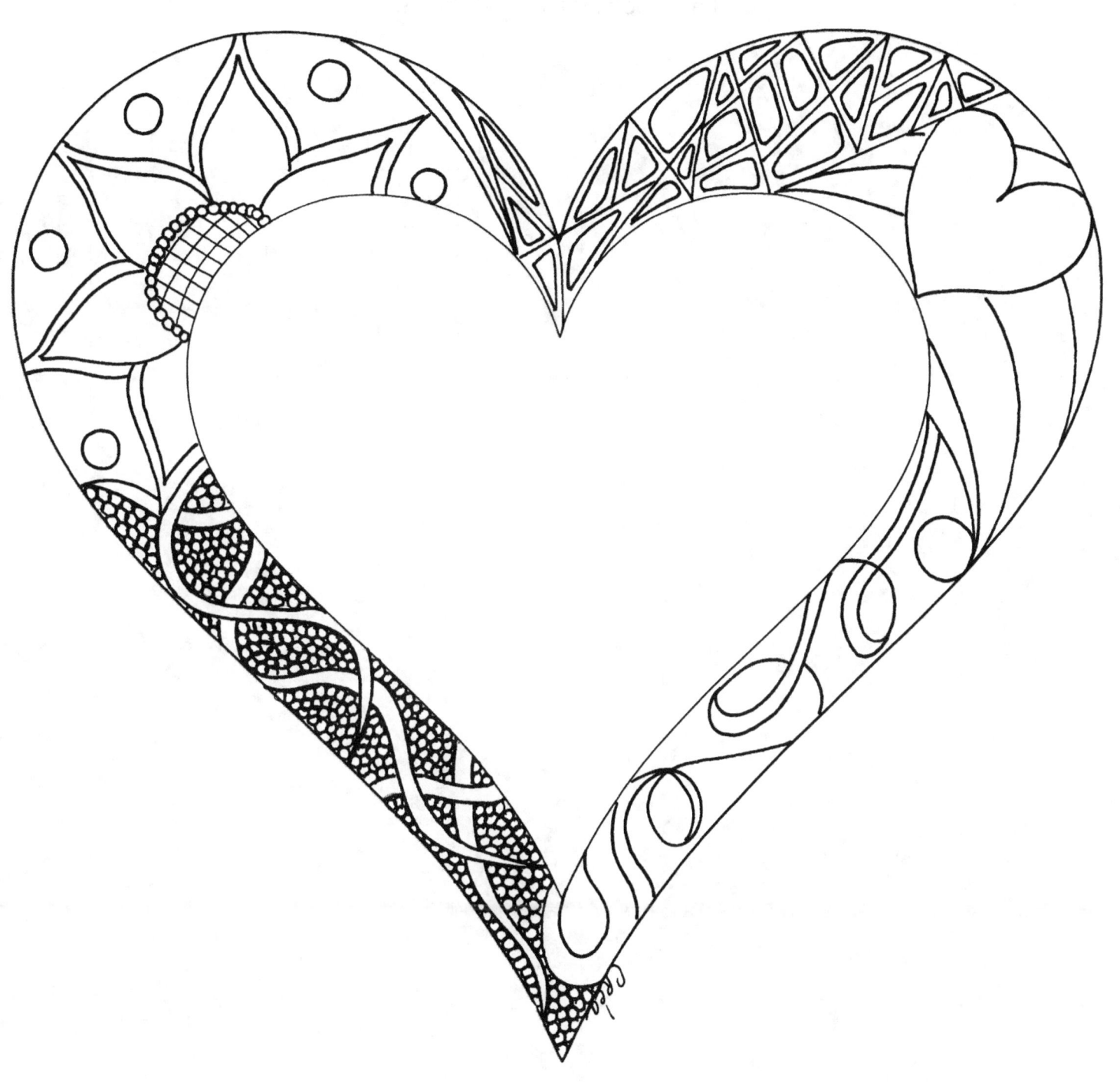

Contributing Artist
Diana Holmes
USA

Facebook : WhimsicalCheers

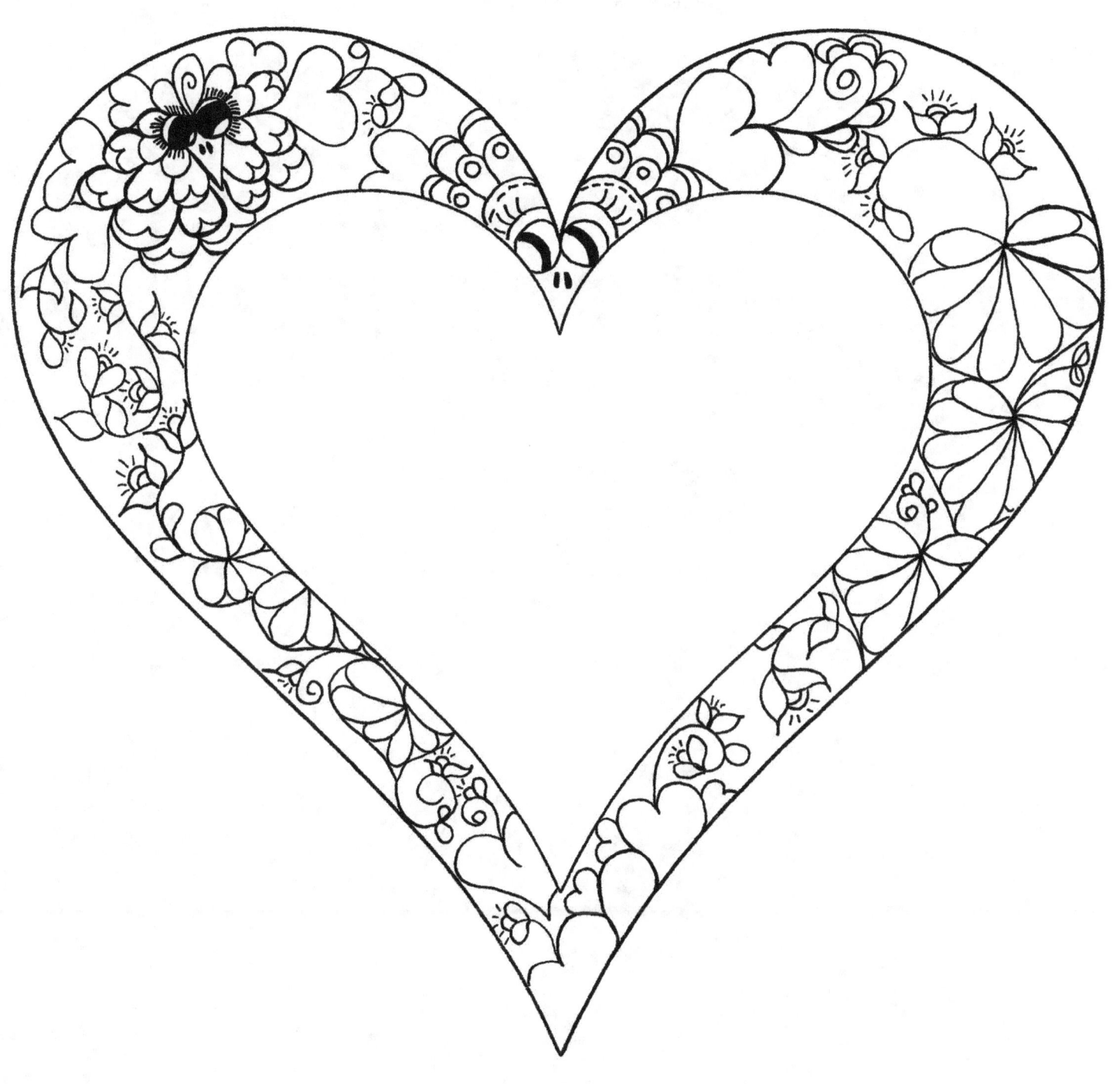

Contributing Artist
Diana Holmes
USA

Facebook : WhimsicalCheers

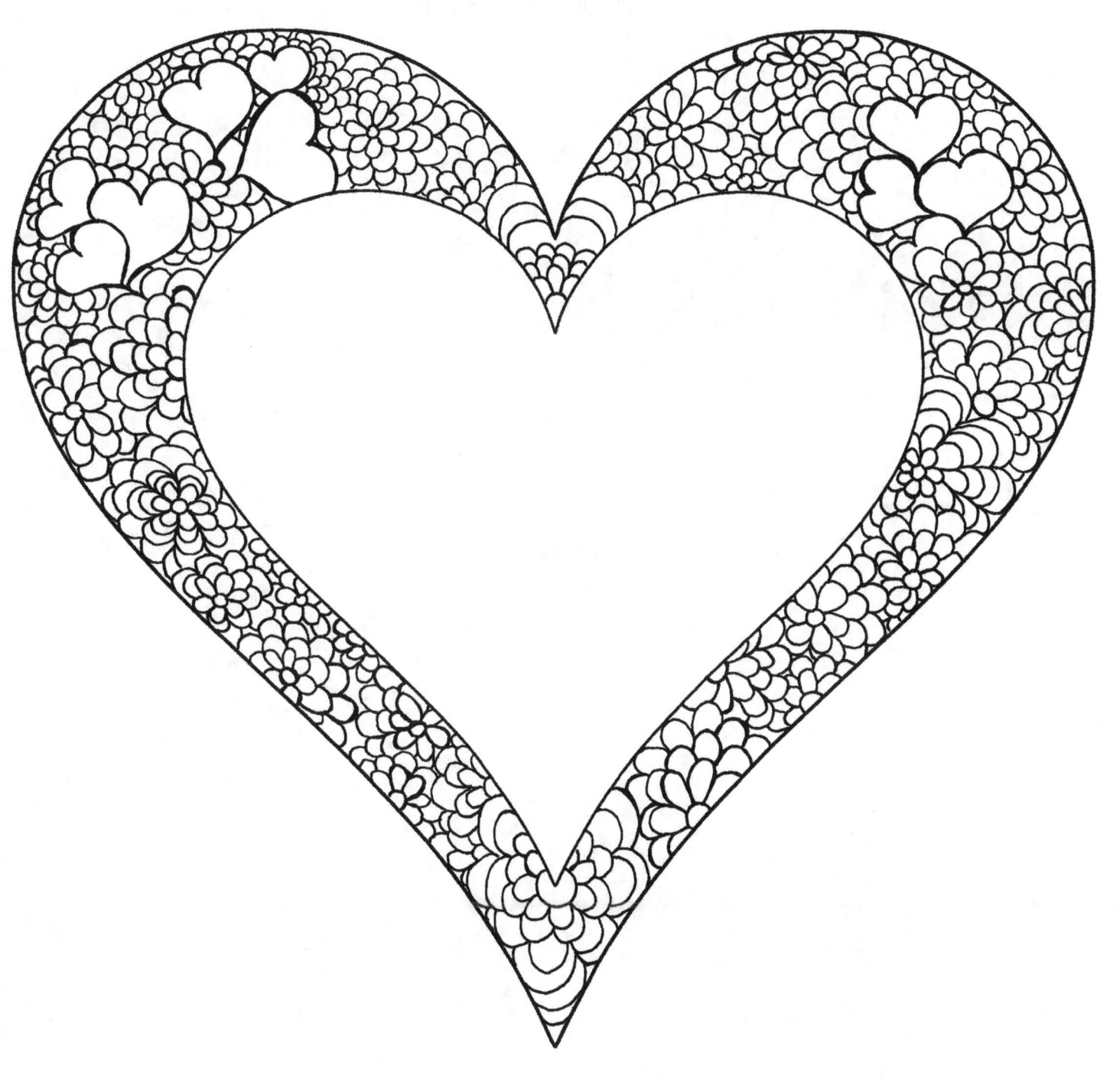

Contributing Artist
Diana Holmes
USA

Facebook : WhimsicalCheers

Contributing Artist
Ellen Wolters
The Netherlands

http://www.tekenpraktijkdeinnerlijkewereld.blogspot.nl/
http://ellenstraties.blogspot.nl/
https://www.youtube.com/user/DIWEllenWolters

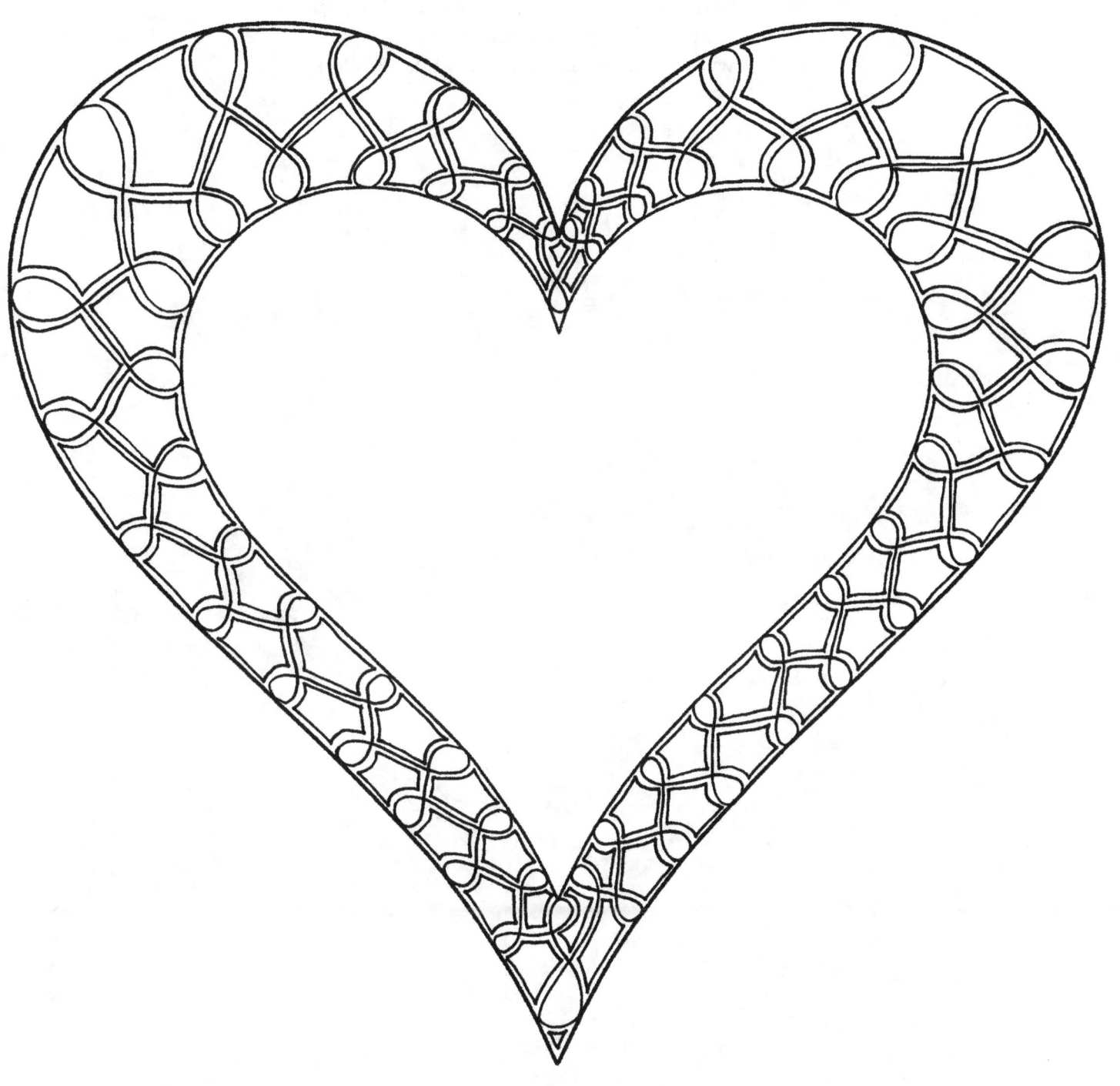

Contributing Artist
Ellen Wolters
The Netherlands

http://www.tekenpraktijkdeinnerlijkewereld.blogspot.nl/
http://ellenstraties.blogspot.nl/
https://www.youtube.com/user/DIWEllenWolters

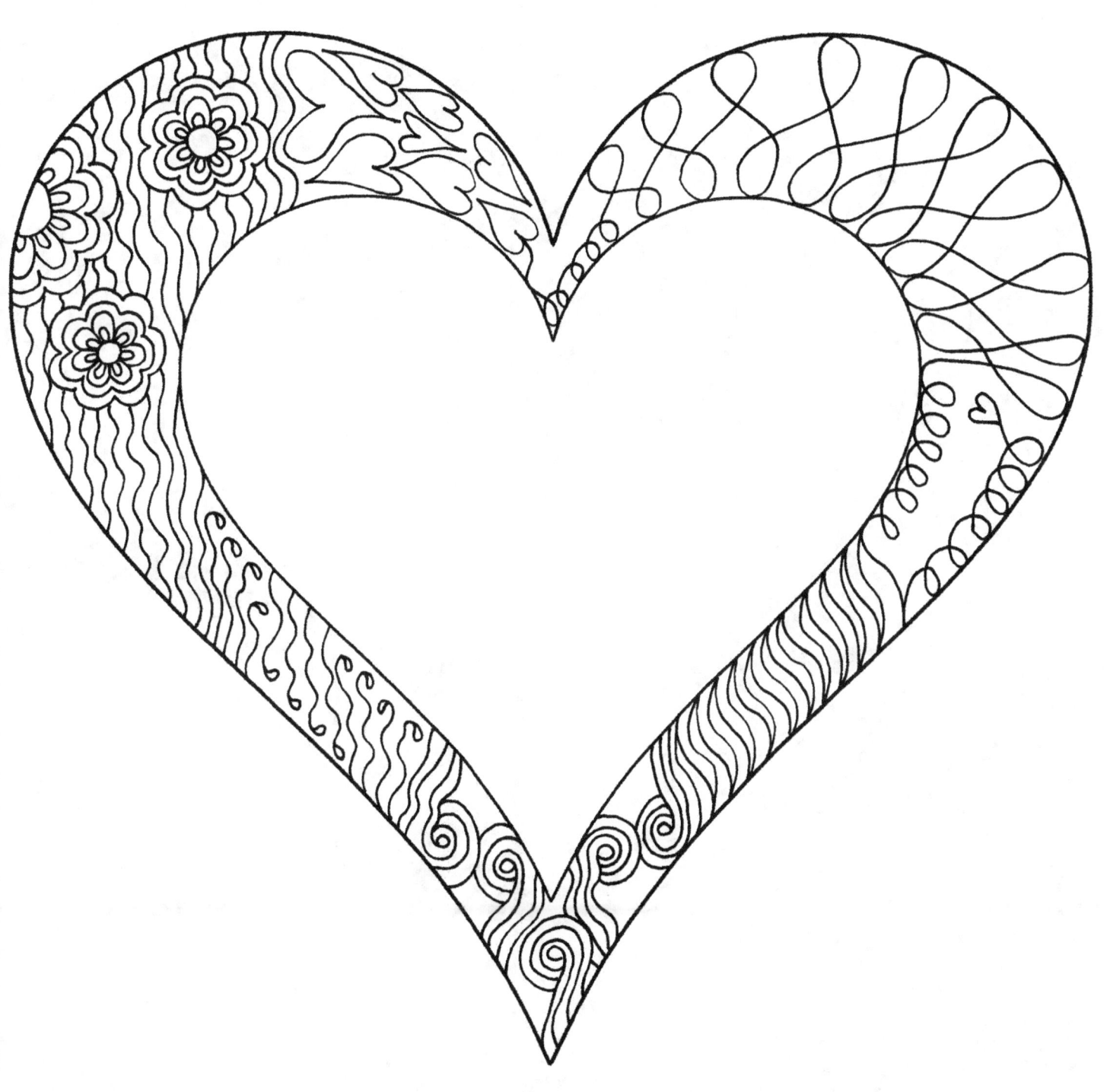

Contributing Artist
Gemeta Ling
Germany

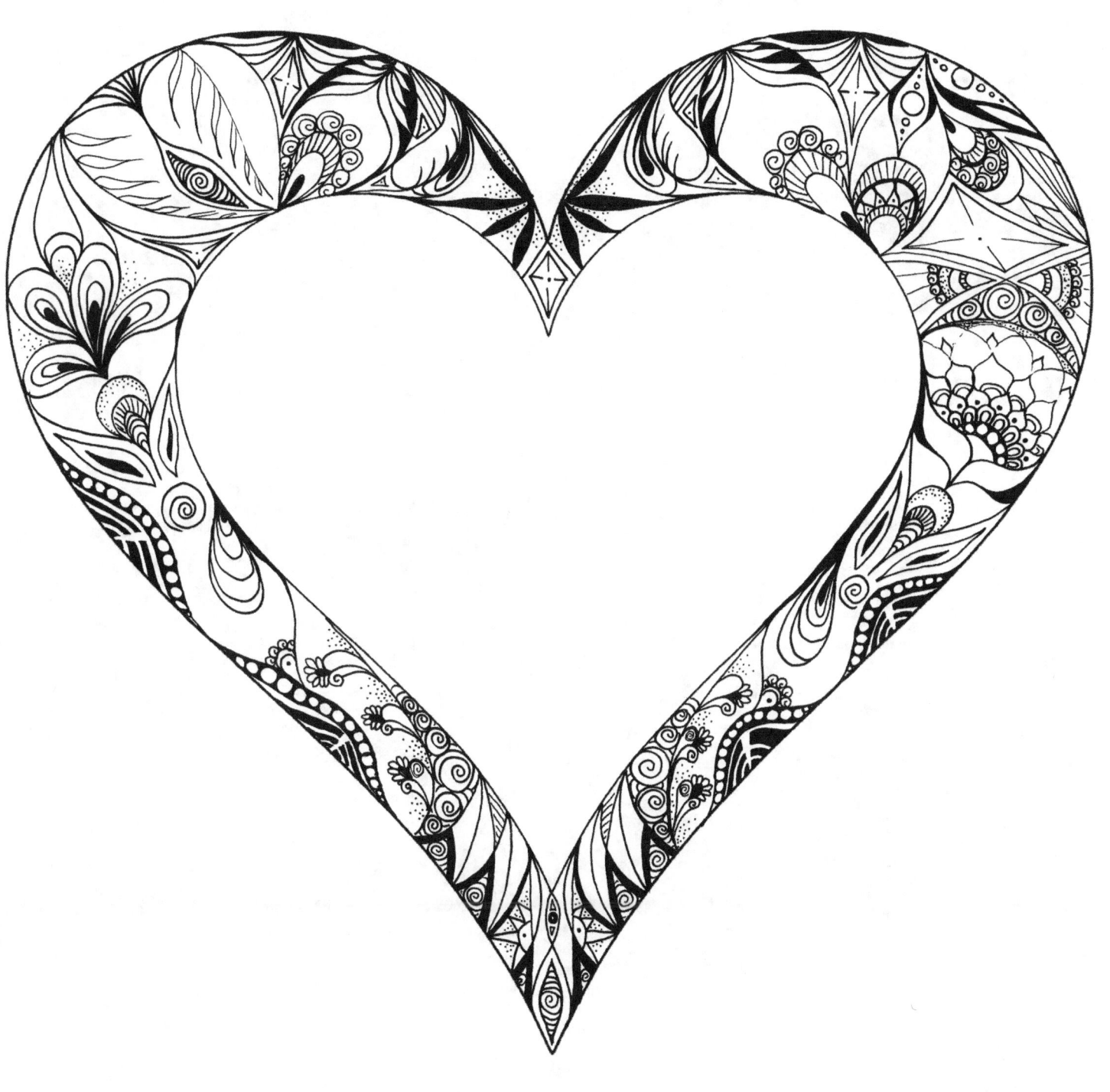

Contributing Artist
Gemeta Ling
Germany

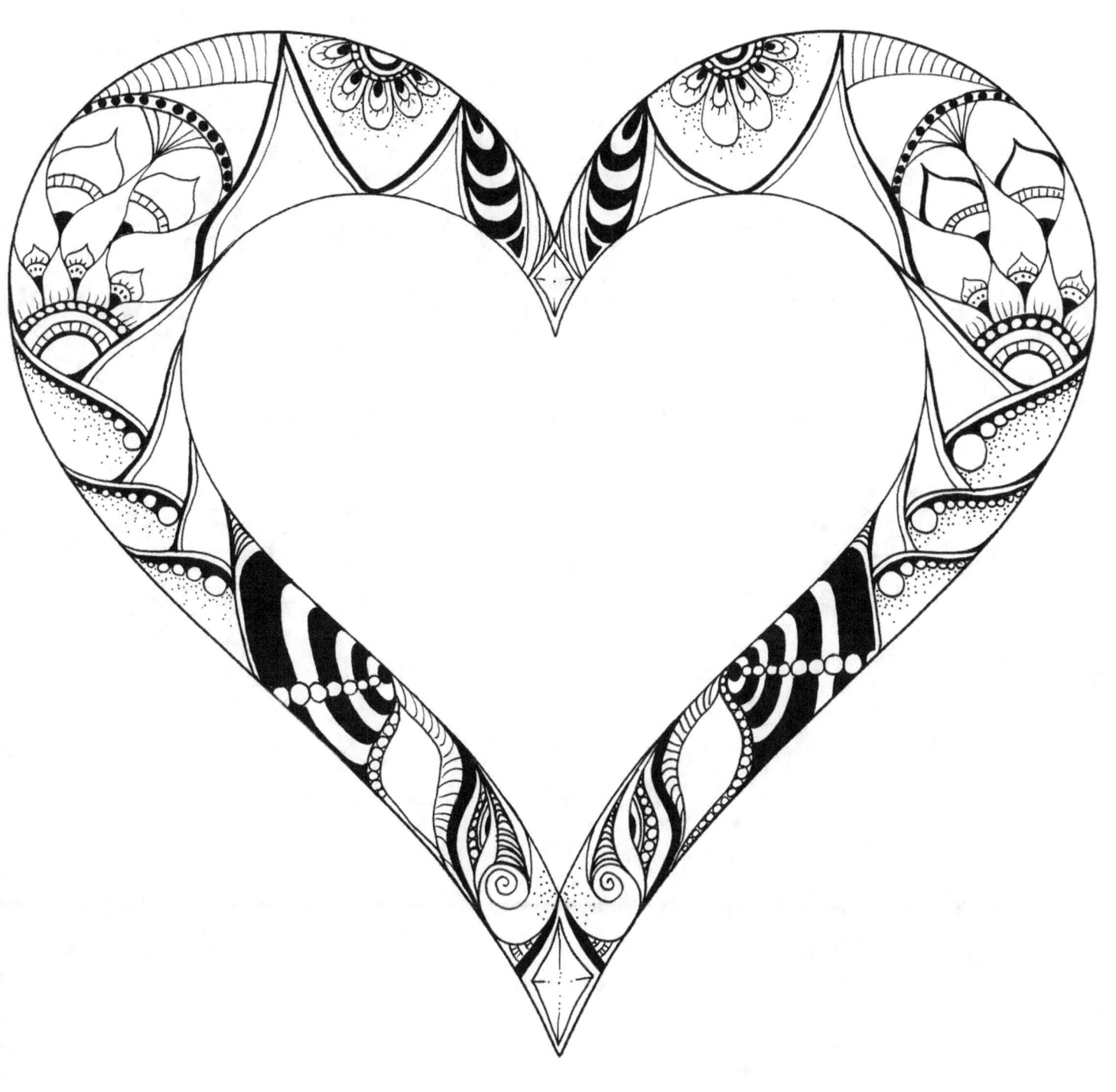

Contributing Artist
Gloria A. Lenzen
USA

Contributing Artist
MWMS-Johanna Ans
The Netherlands

Blog : mywaymystylejohannaans.wordpress.com

Facebook : Johanna-Ans-My-creative-site

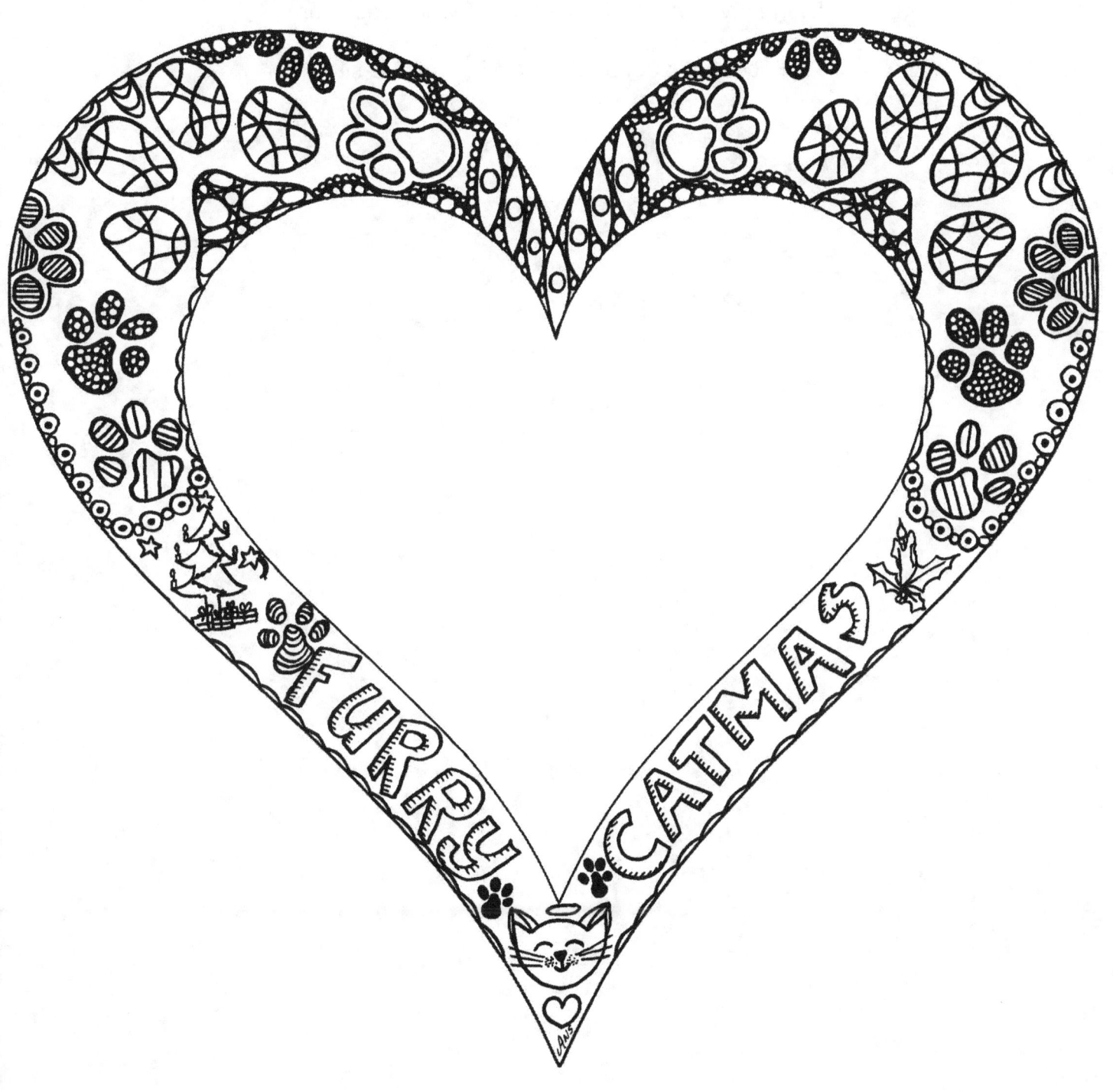

Contributing Artist
MWMS-Johanna Ans
The Netherlands

Blog : mywaymystylejohannaans.wordpress.com

Facebook : Johanna-Ans-My-creative-site

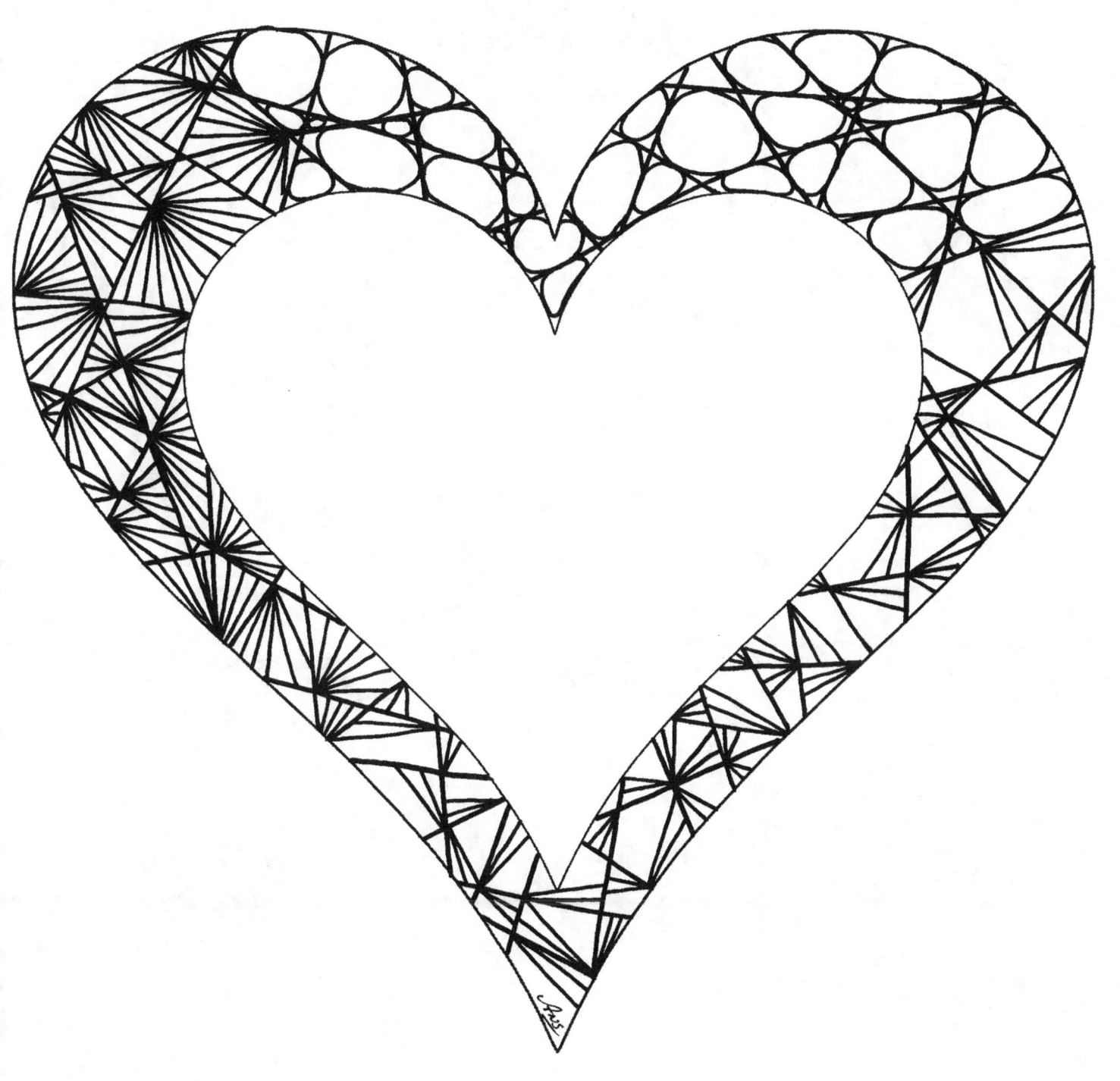

Contributing Artist
Kaloo Design
France

Facebook : Ka LooDesign
Twitter : Kaloo Design

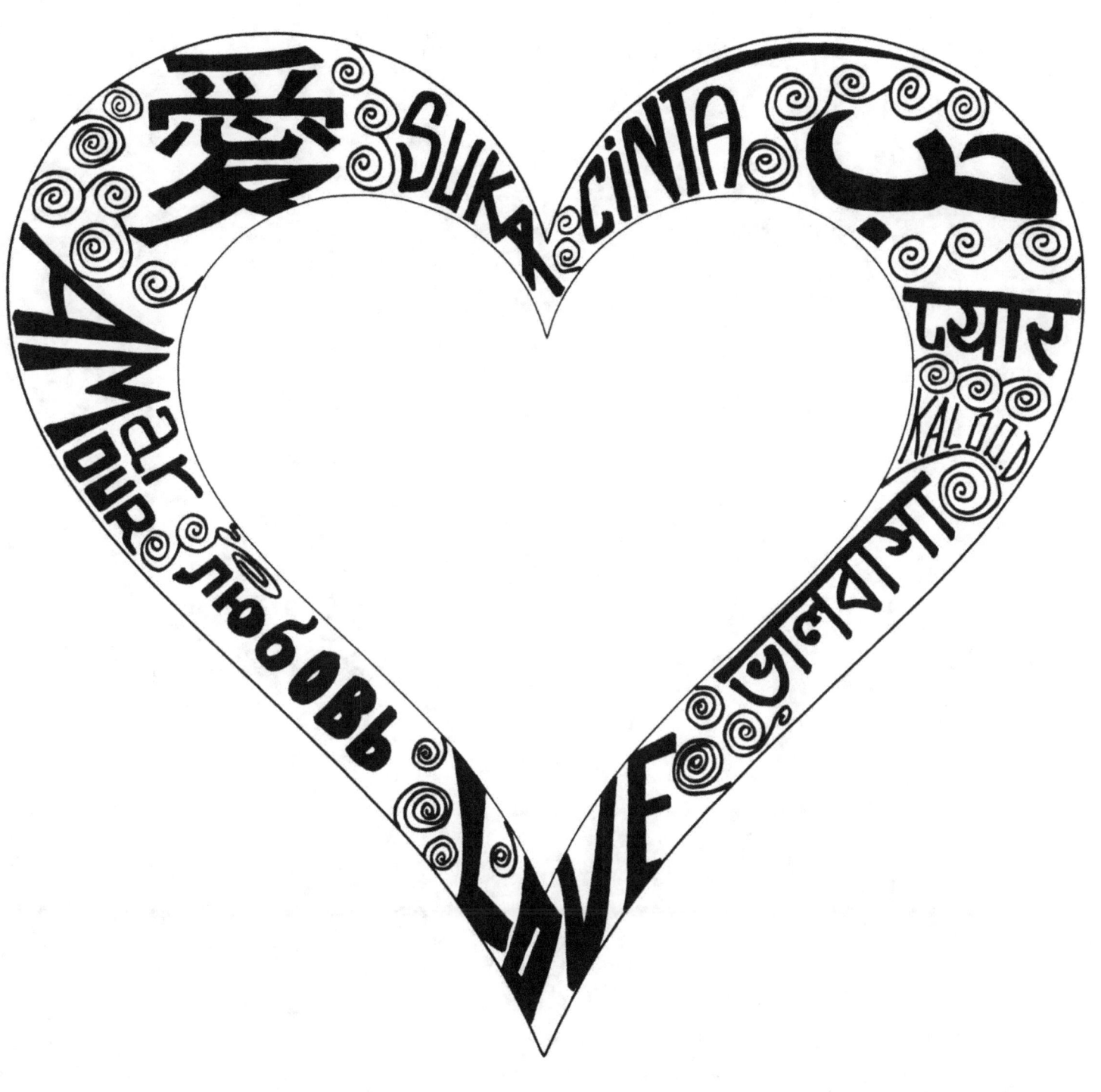

Contributing Artist
Lilan Chen
Taiwan

Facebook : lilanchen.art

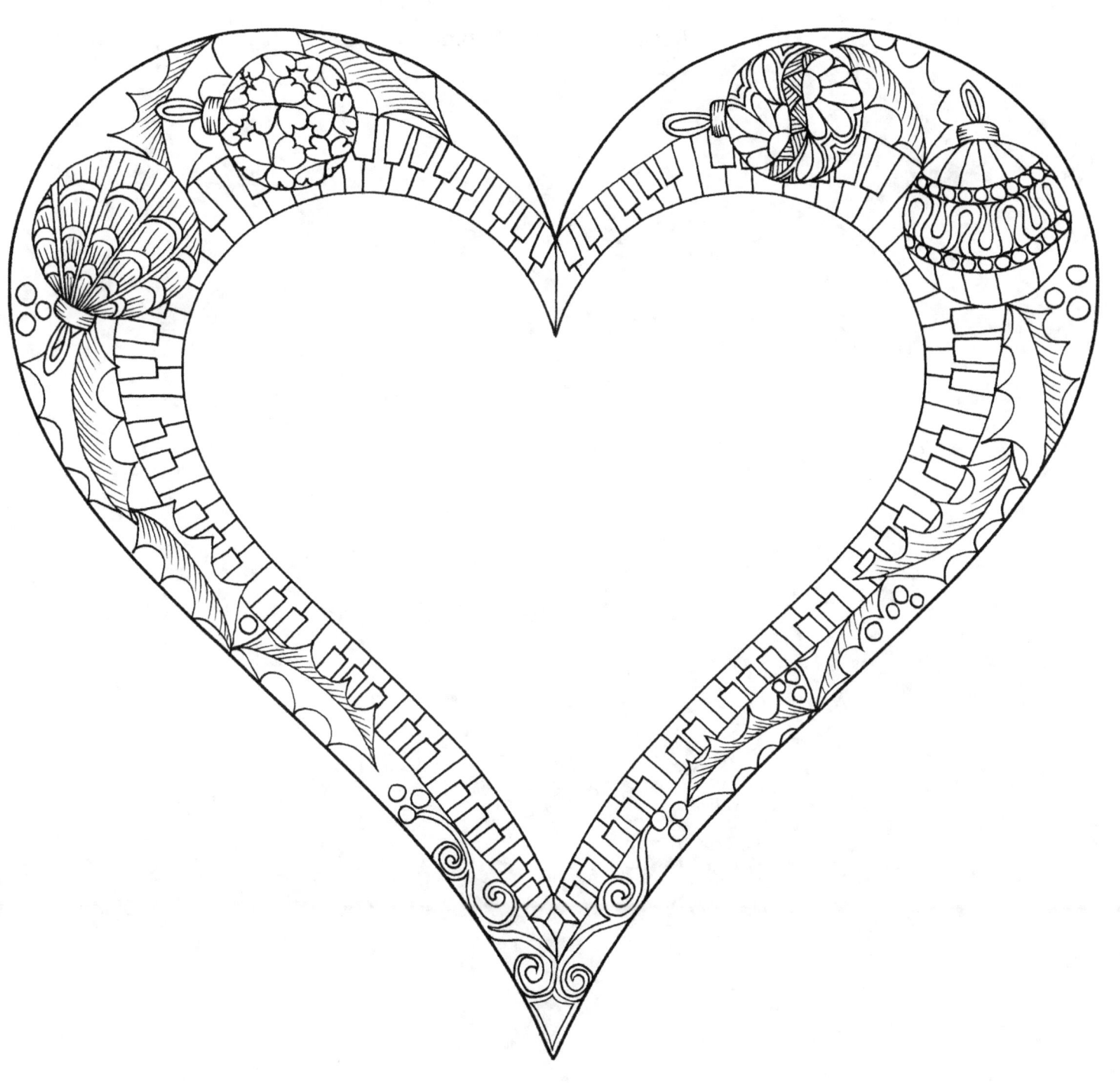

Contributing Artist
Lilan Chen
Taiwan

Facebook : lilanchen.art

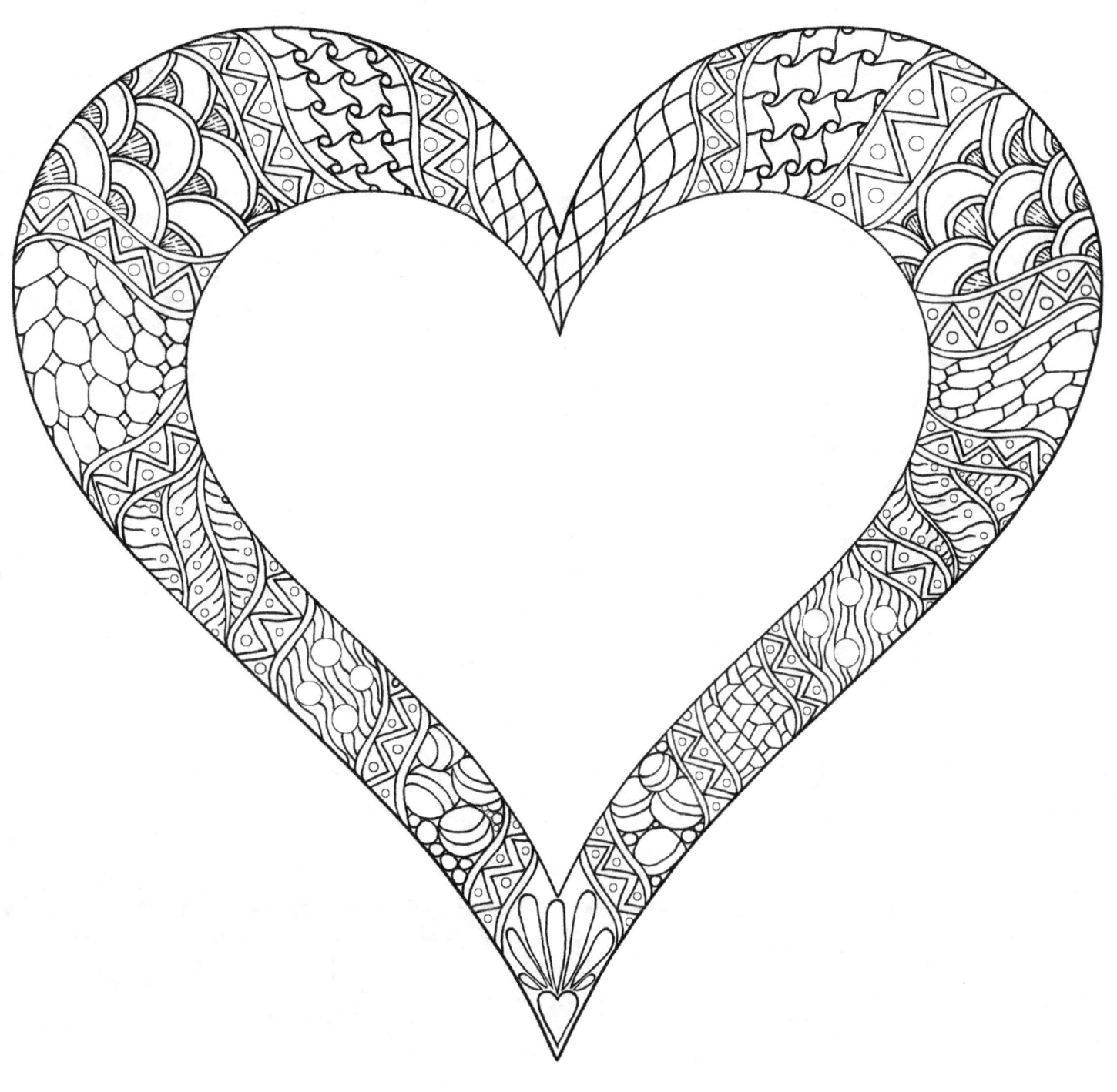

Contributing Artist
Lynne McGee
Brisbane, Australia

Facebook : Colorandtangle

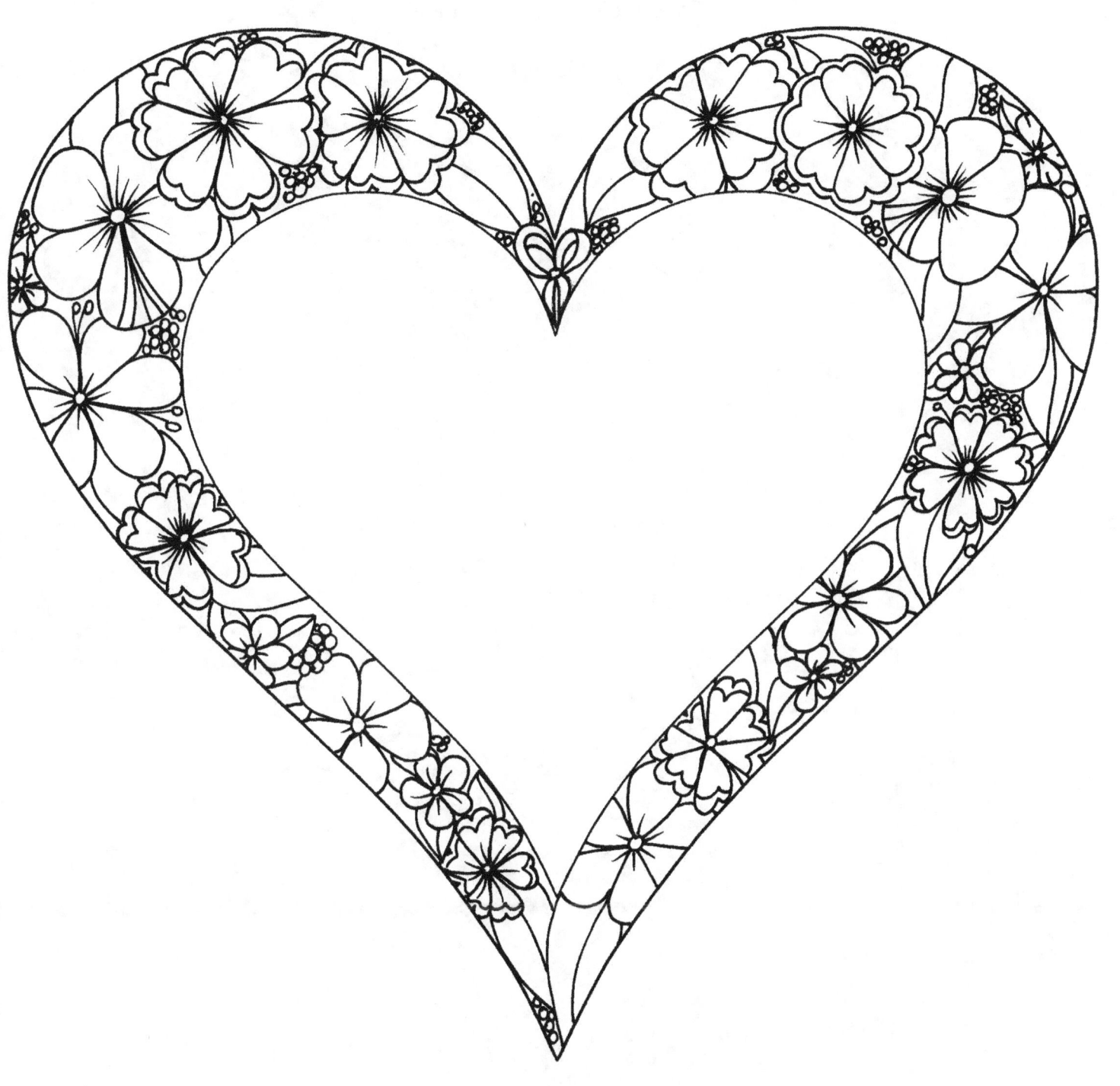

Contributing Artist
Lynne McGee
Brisbane, Australia

Facebook : Colorandtangle

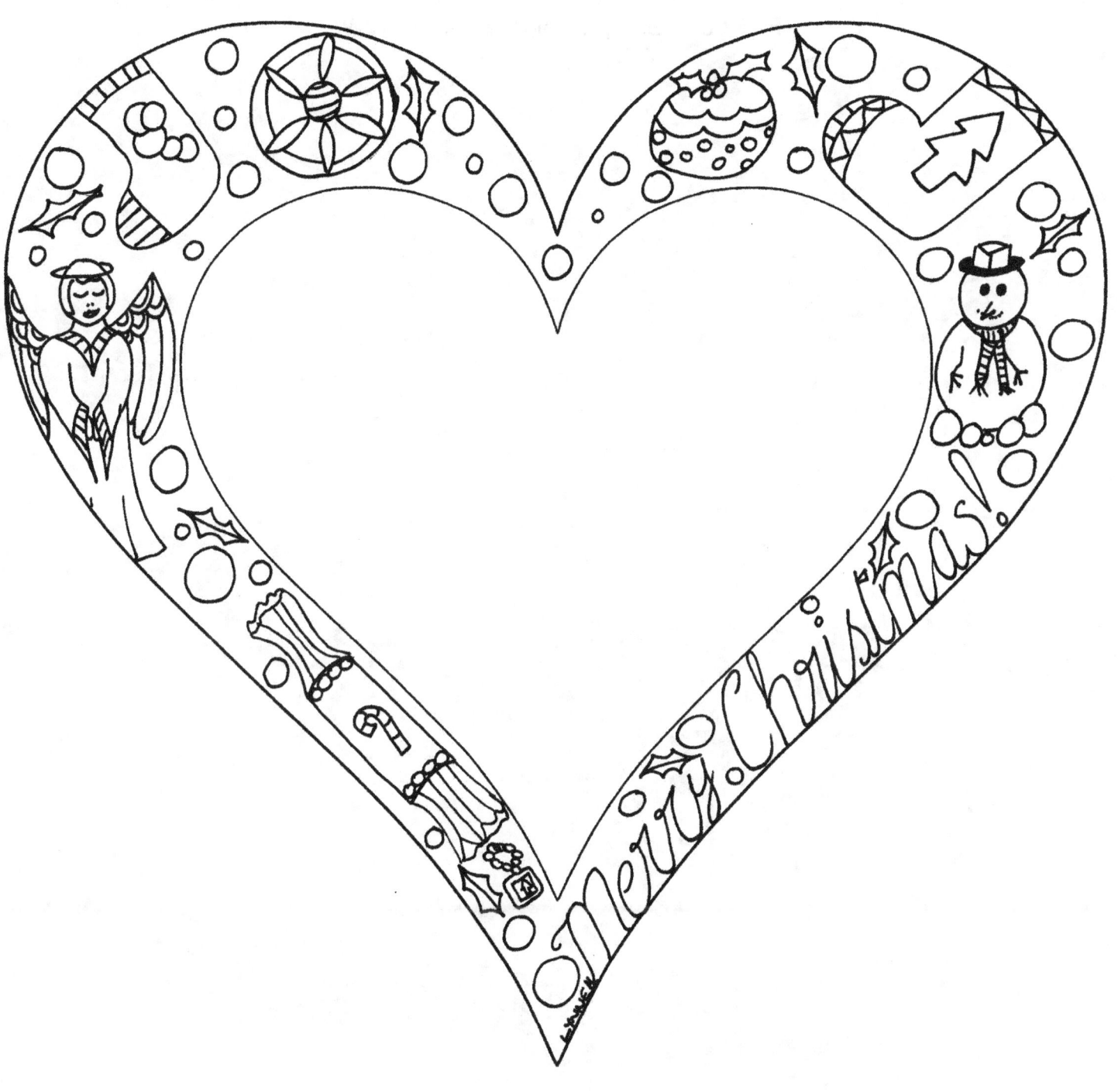

Contributing Artist
Maria Wedel
Denmark

Facebook : AMVWART
Facebook Group : ColorPagesOfAMVW/

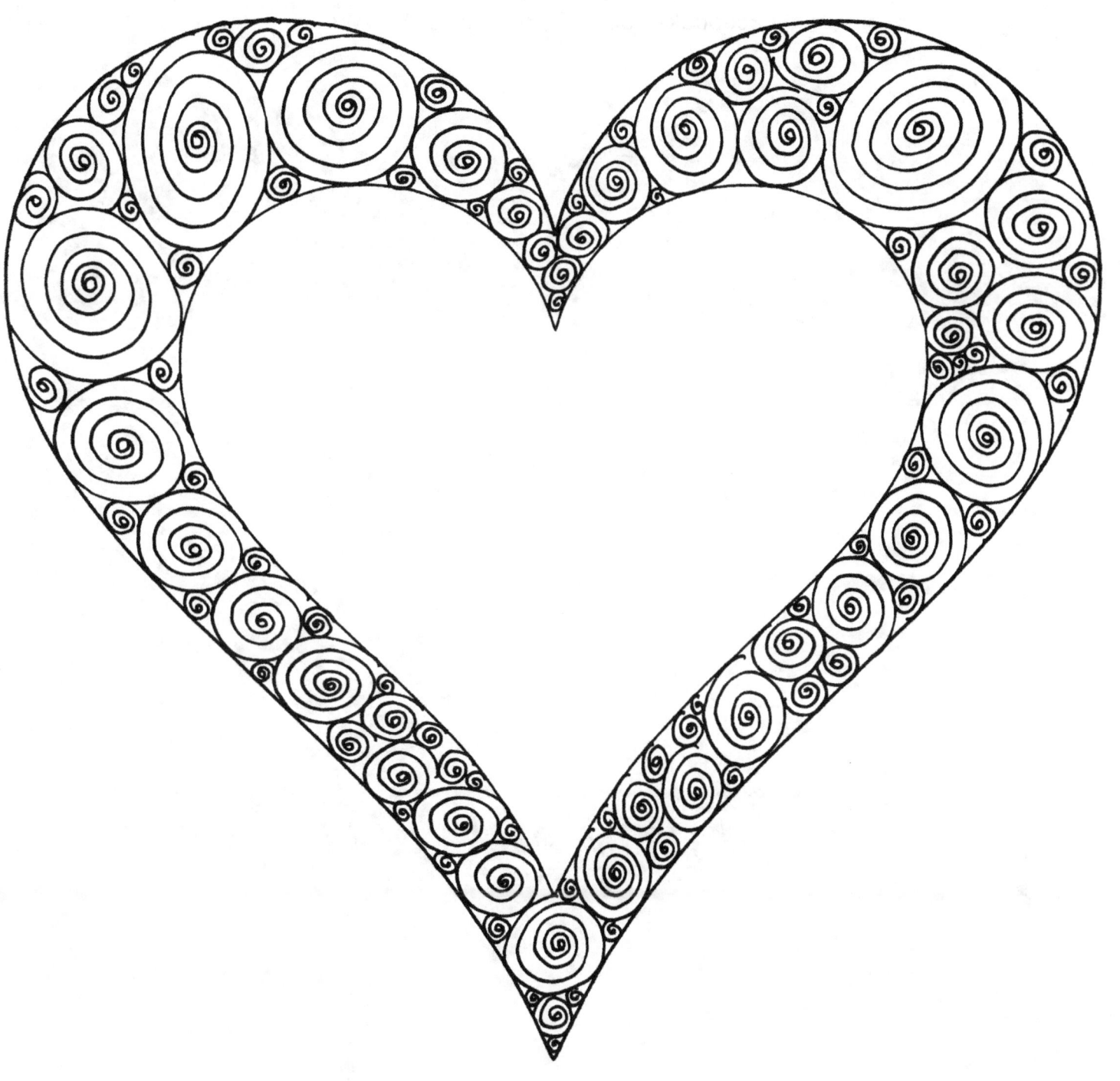

Contributing Artist
Maria Wedel
Denmark

Facebook : AMVWART
Facebook Group : ColorPagesOfAMVW/

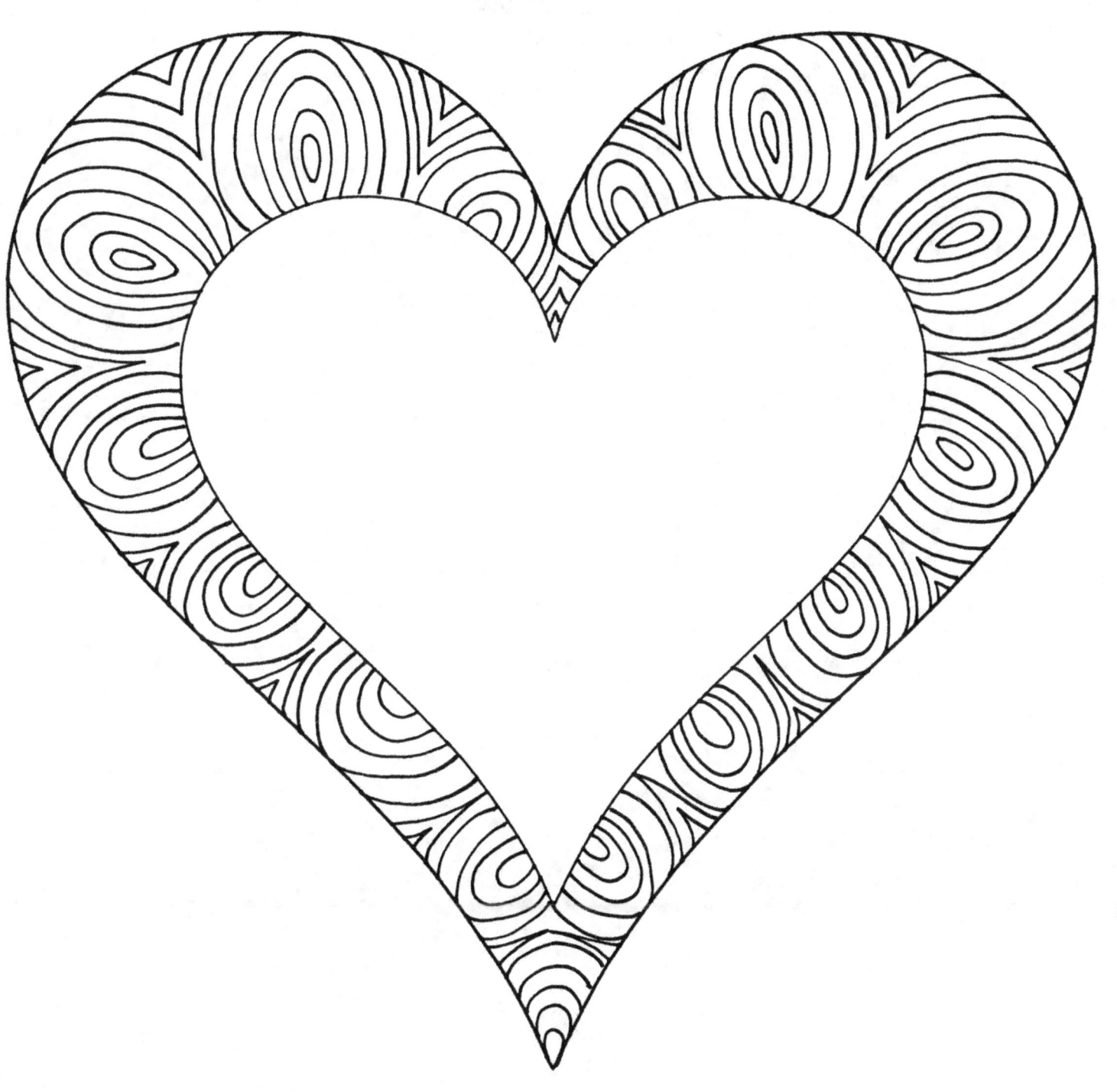

Contributing Artist
Maria Wedel
Denmark

Facebook : AMVWART
Facebook Group : ColorPagesOfAMVW/

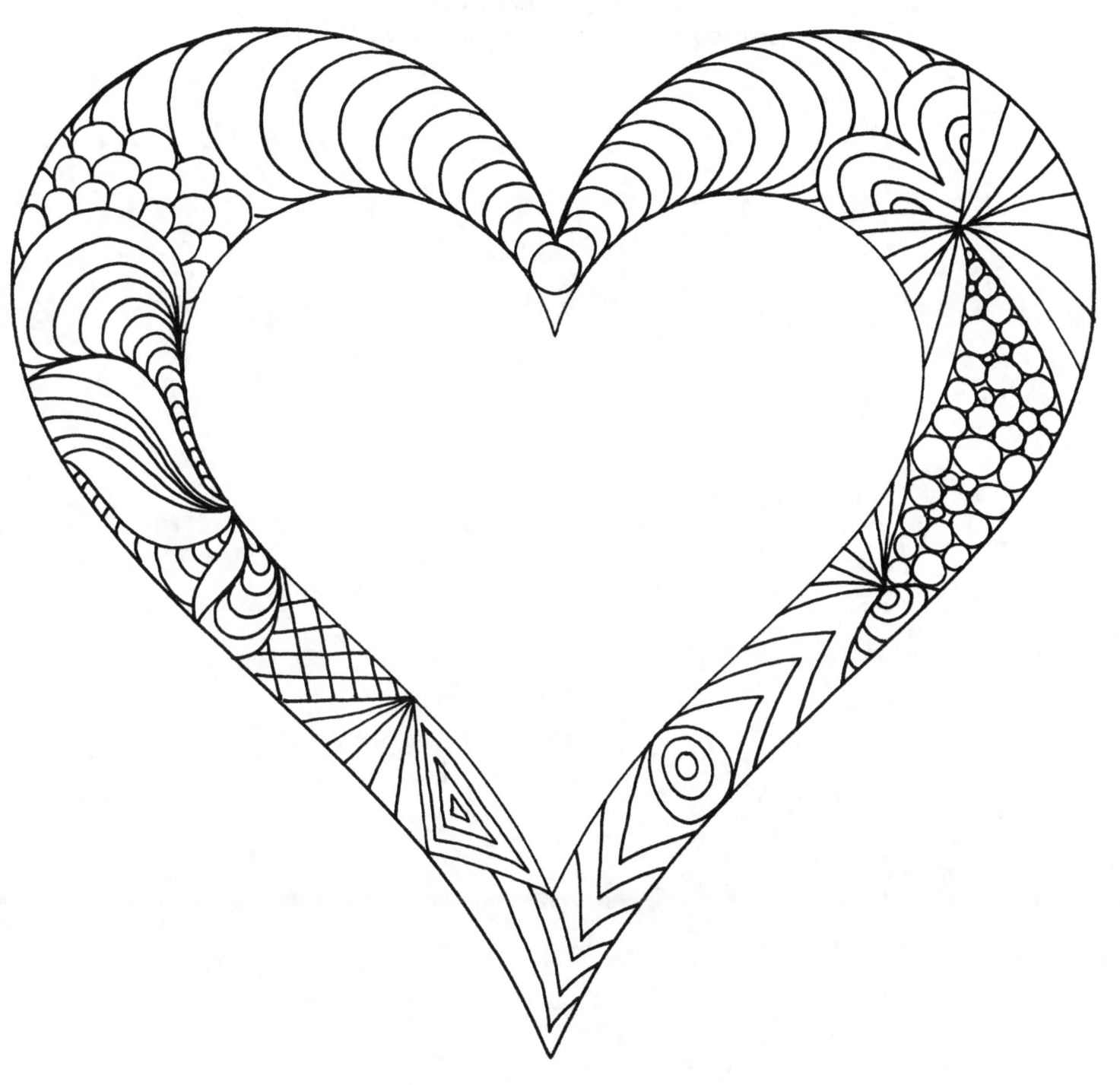

Contributing Artist
Maria Wedel
Denmark

Facebook : AMVWART
Facebook Group : ColorPagesOfAMVW/

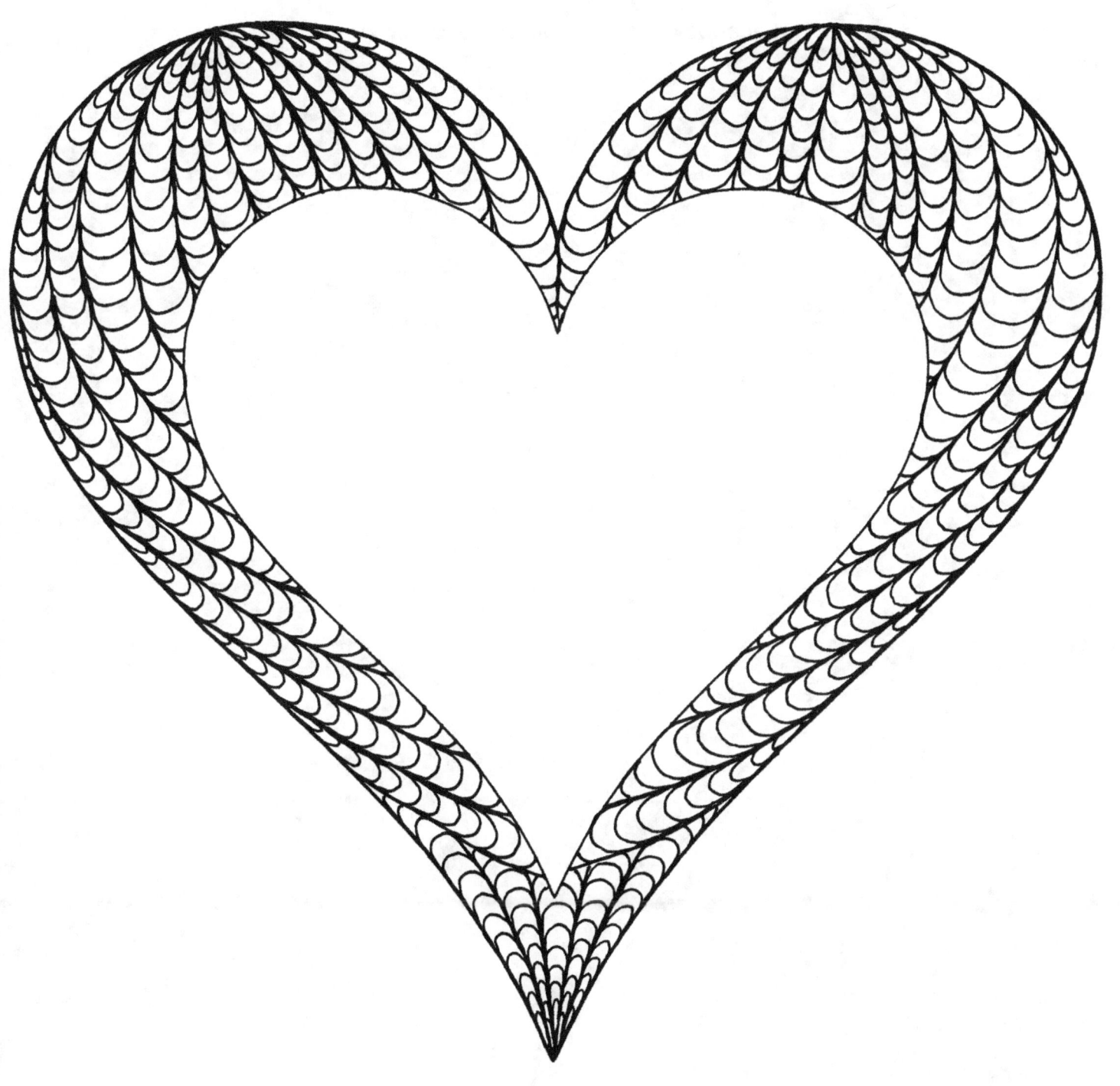

Contributing Artist
Maria Wedel
Denmark

Facebook : AMVWART
Facebook Group : ColorPagesOfAMVW/

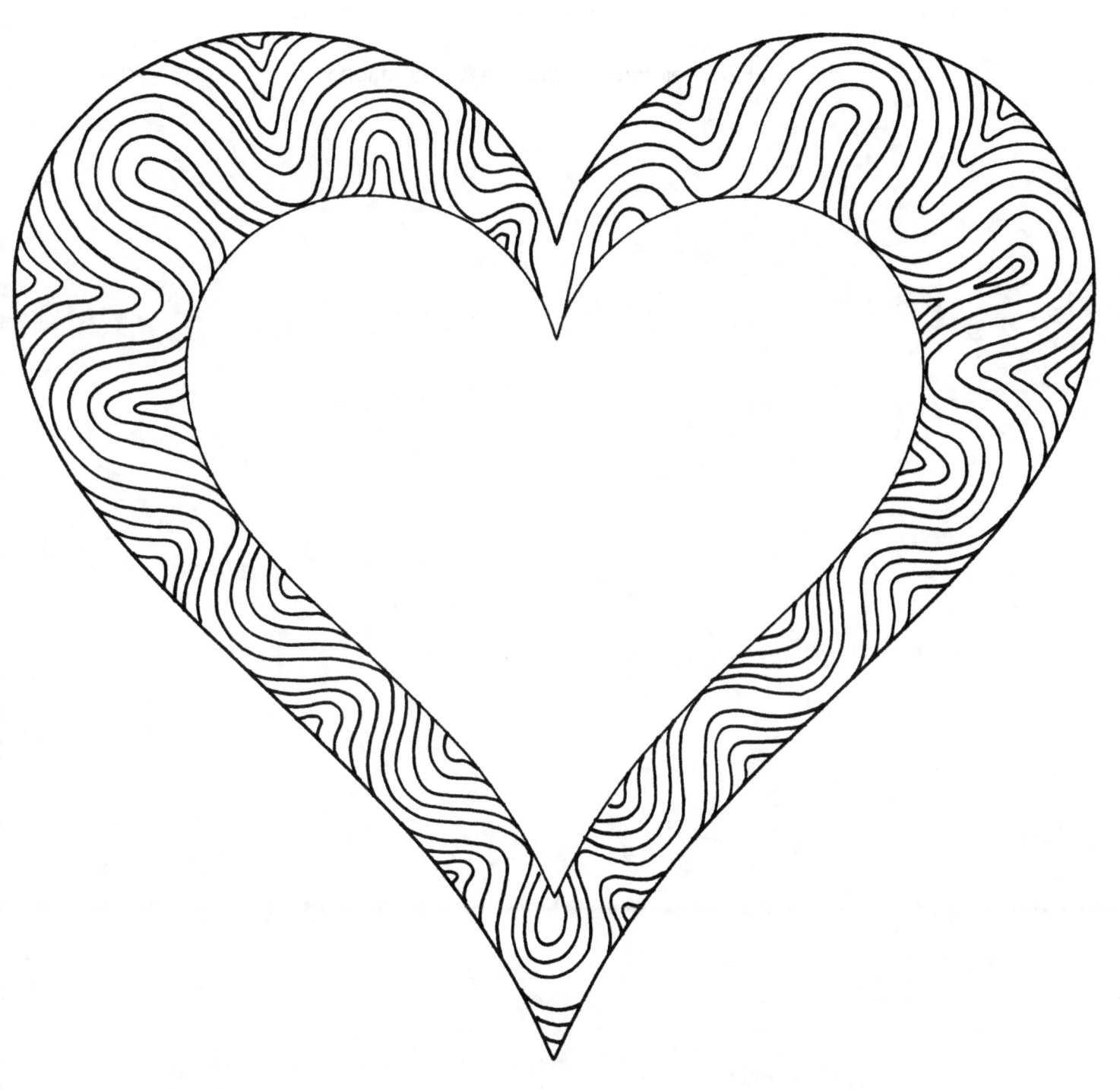

Contributing Artist
Maud Feral Chauveau
(MFC)
France

« MFC - Peinture, graphisme & illustration »

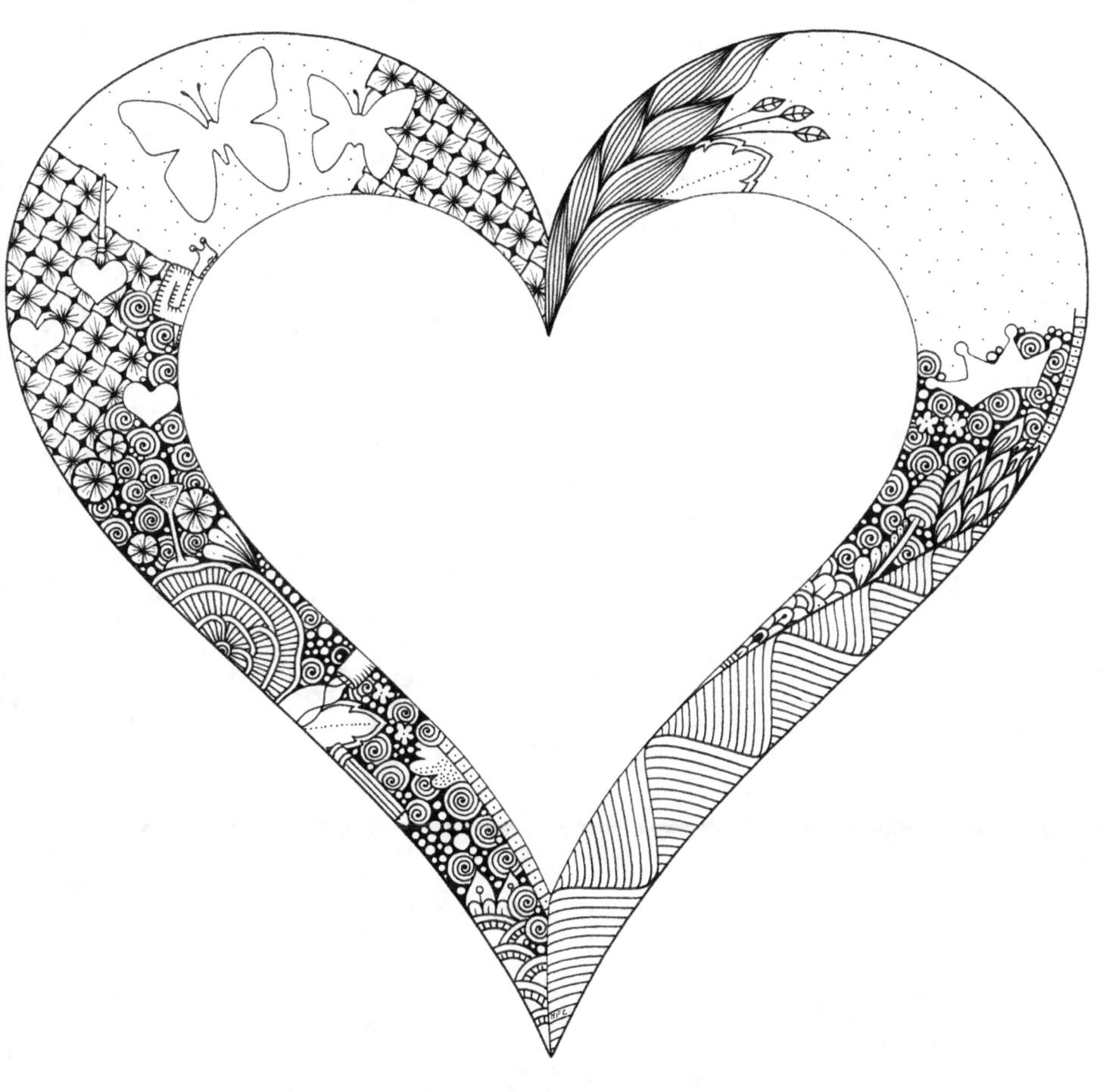

Contributing Artist
Maud Feral Chauveau
(MFC)
France

« MFC - Peinture, graphisme & illustration »

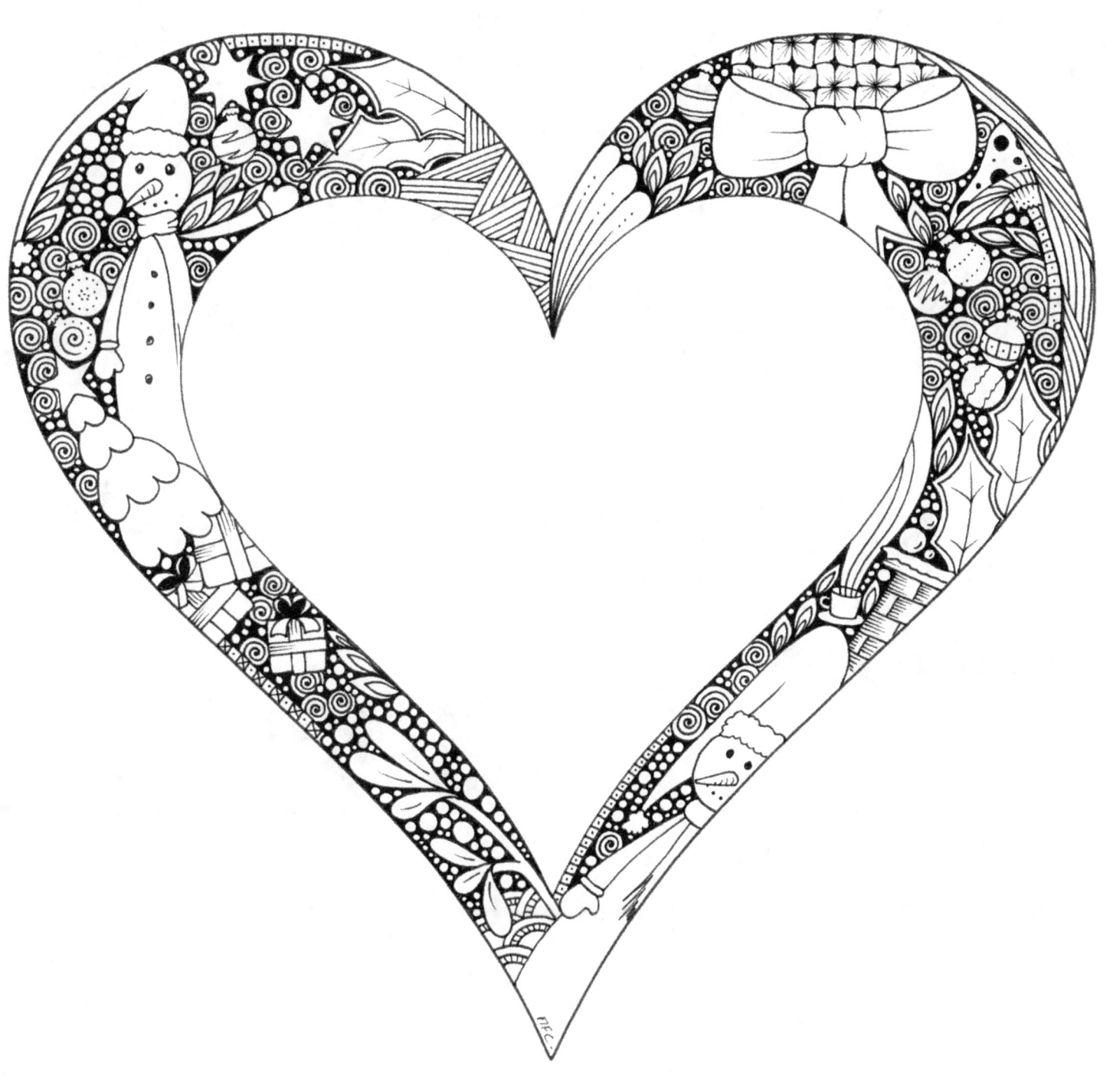

Contributing Artist
Neeti Goswami
Canada

www.artbyneeti.ca

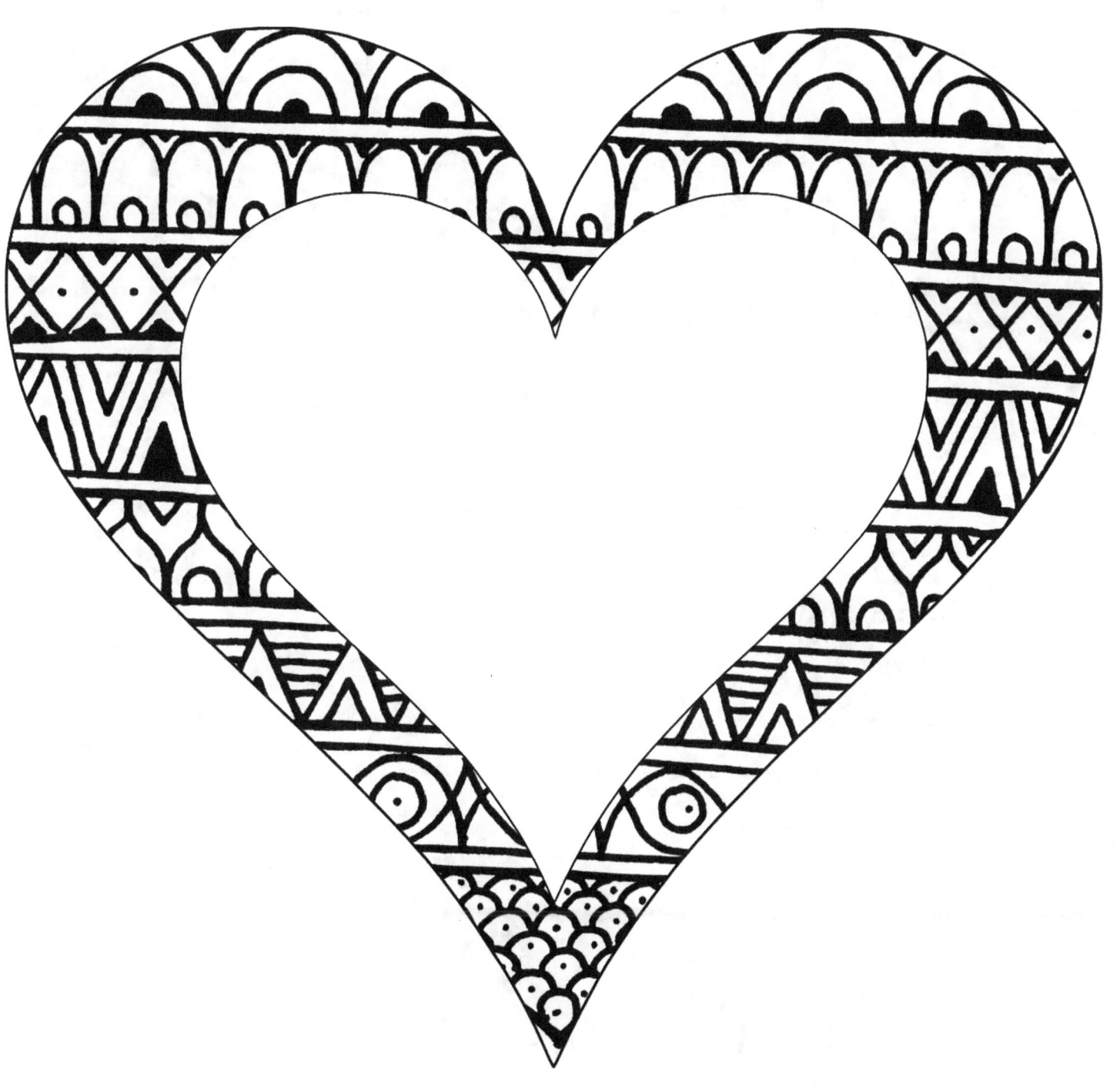

Contributing Artist
Mireille Westerduin, Colour by Mi
The Netherlands

Facebook : Colour-by-Mi-Kleurplaten-Illustraties

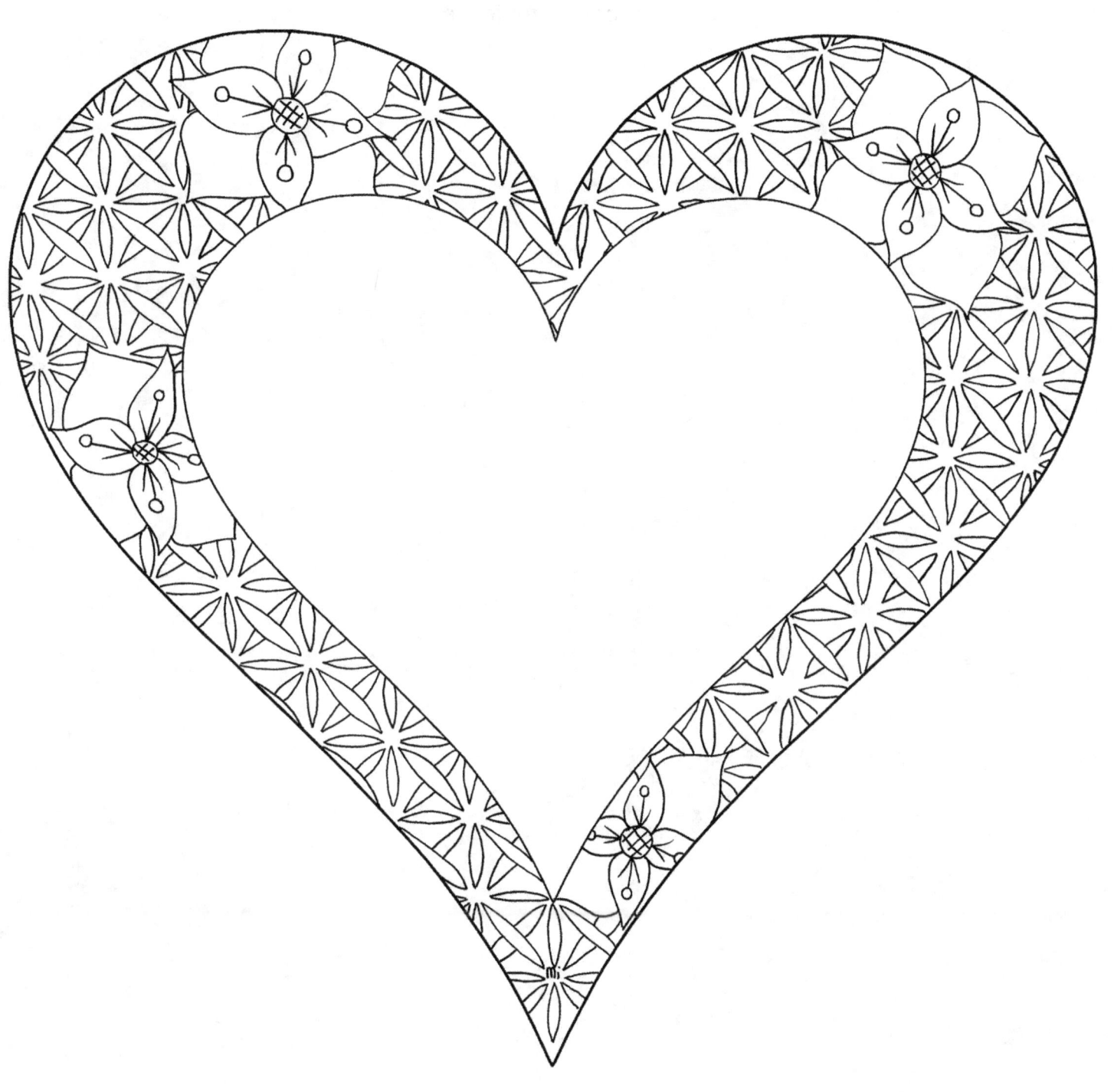

Contributing Artist
Nadège Zenfeerie
France

Facebook : zenfeerie

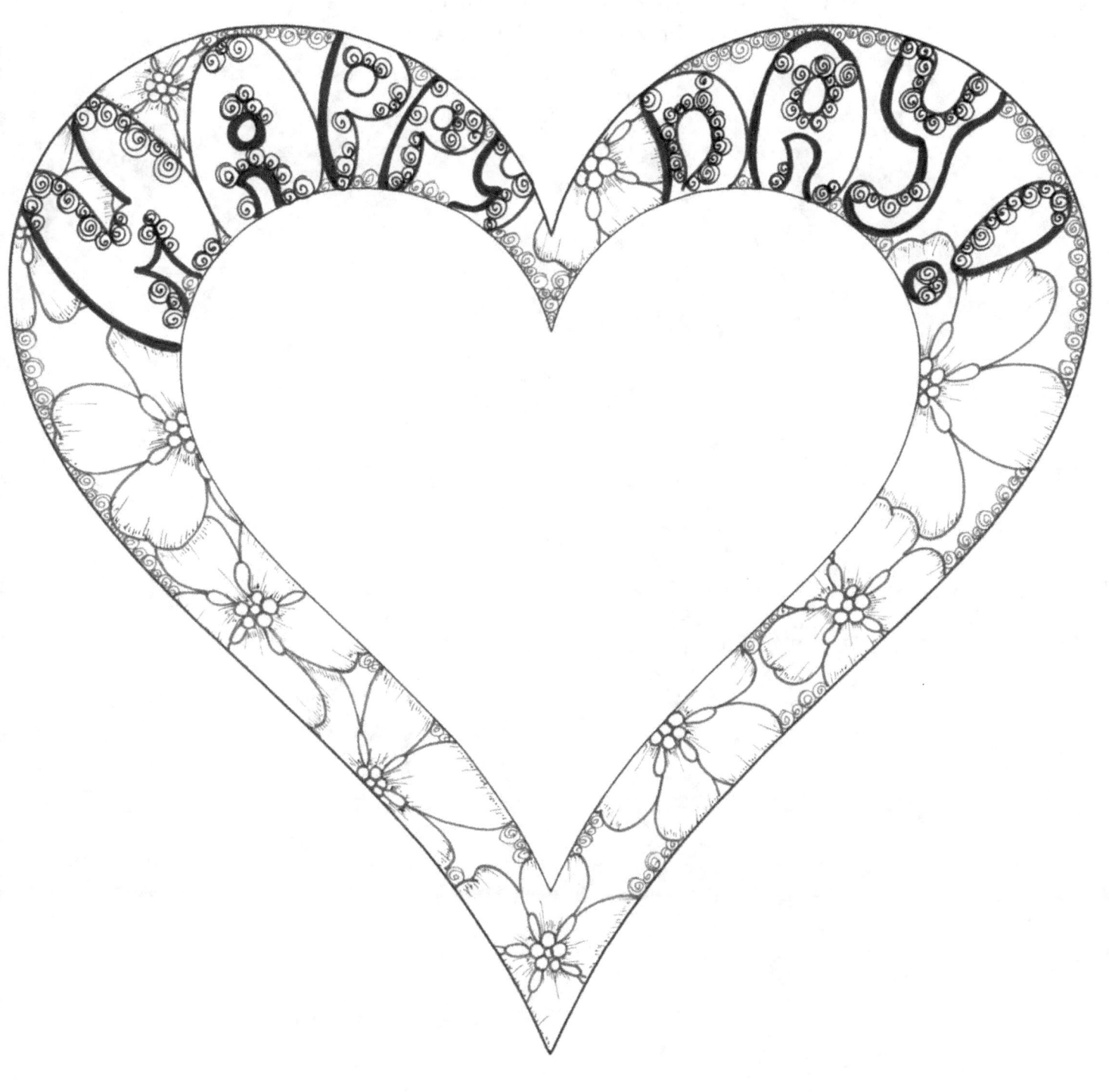

Contributing Artist
Nicole Whelan (Willow Hill Art)
WI, USA

Facebook : WillowHillArt
Etsy shop : WillowHillArt

Contributing Artist
Sabine Design
The Netherlands

Facebook : Sabine-Design

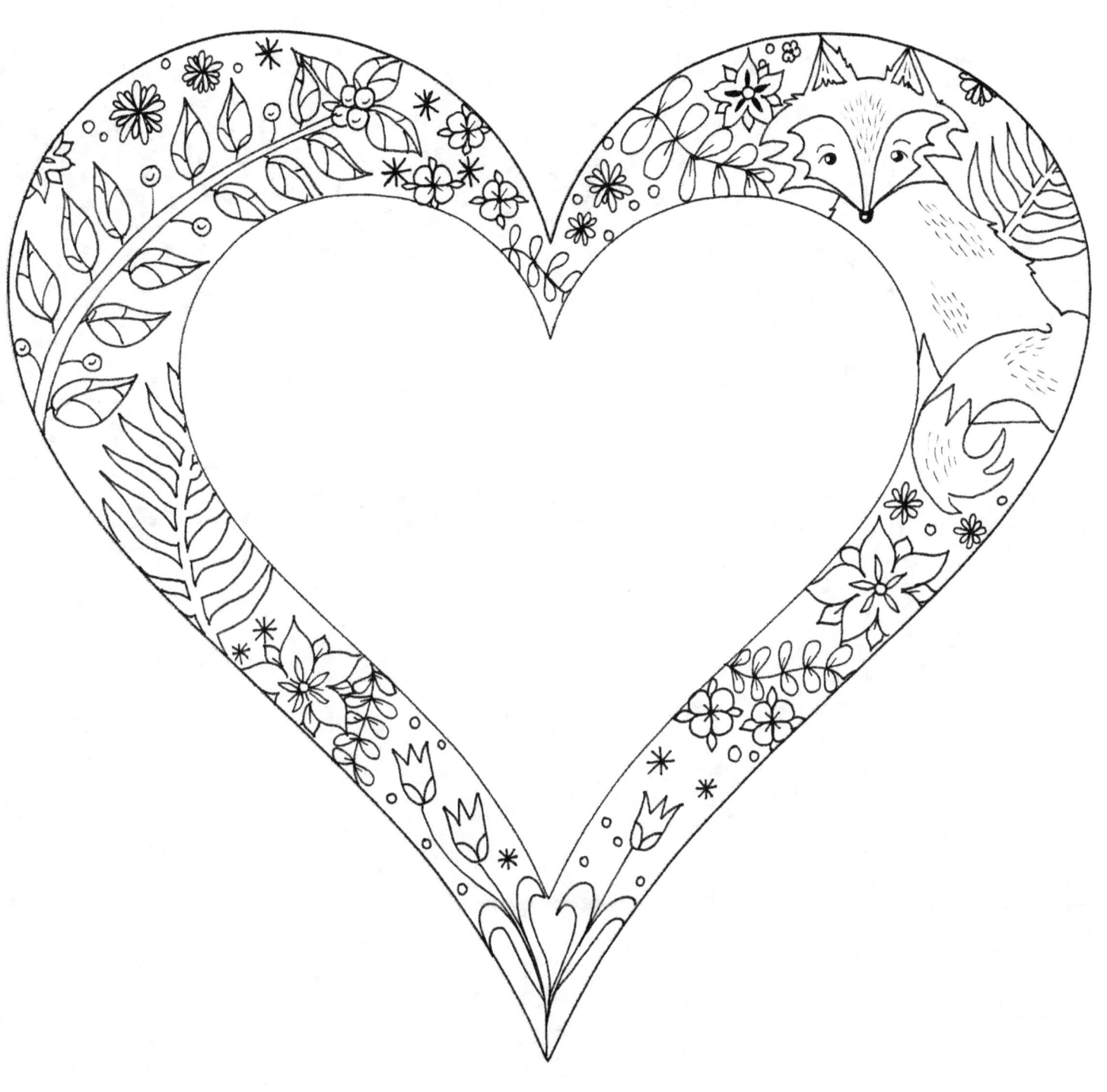

Contributing Artist
Sabine Design
The Netherlands

Facebook : Sabine-Design

Contributing Artist
Tamara A. Cameron
USA

www.colorbinge.com
http://colorbinge.myshopify.com
Facebook : ColorBinge2

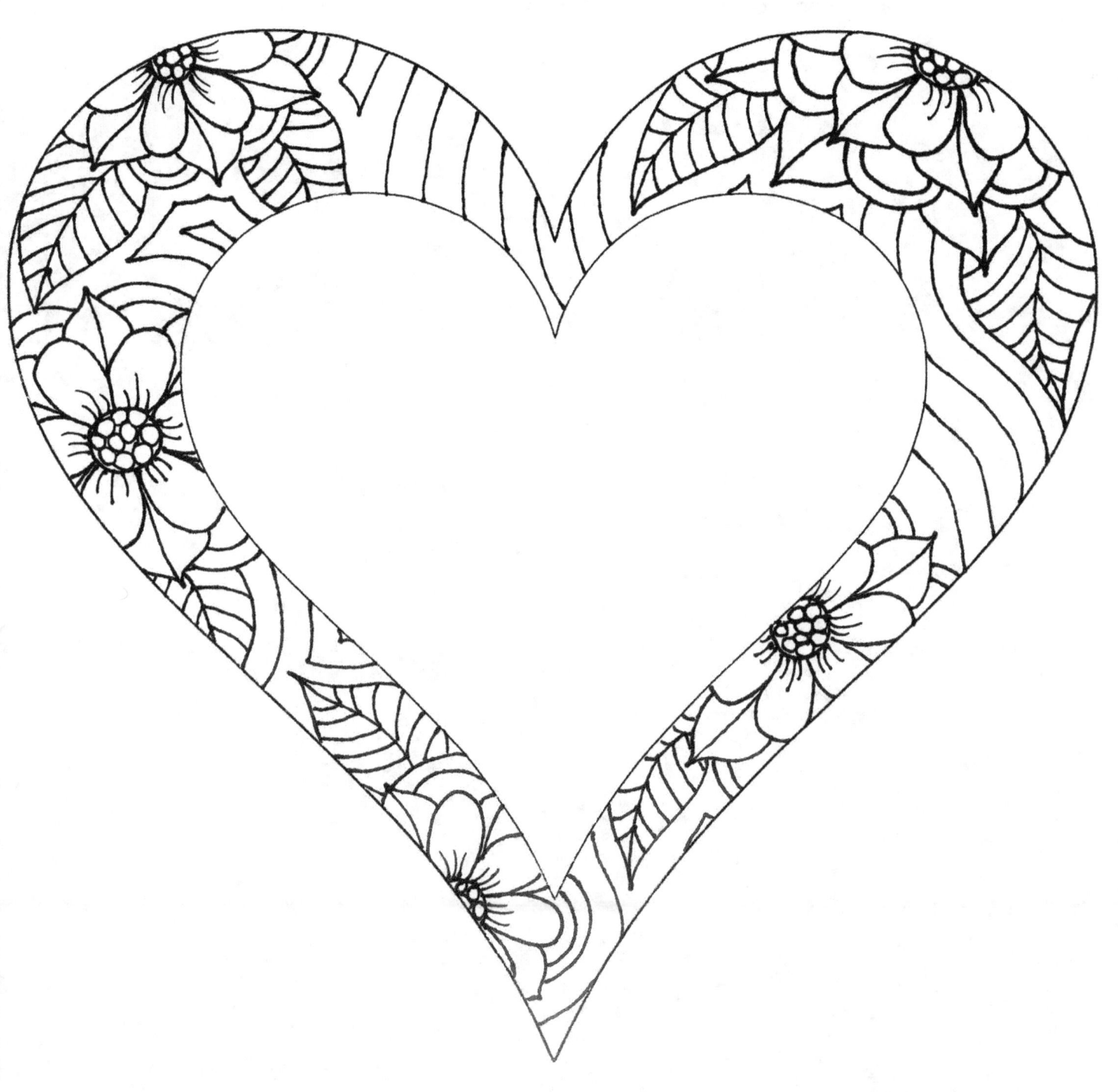

Contributing Artist
Yaya
France

Facebook : Les-gribouillis-de-yaya-georgia-merino

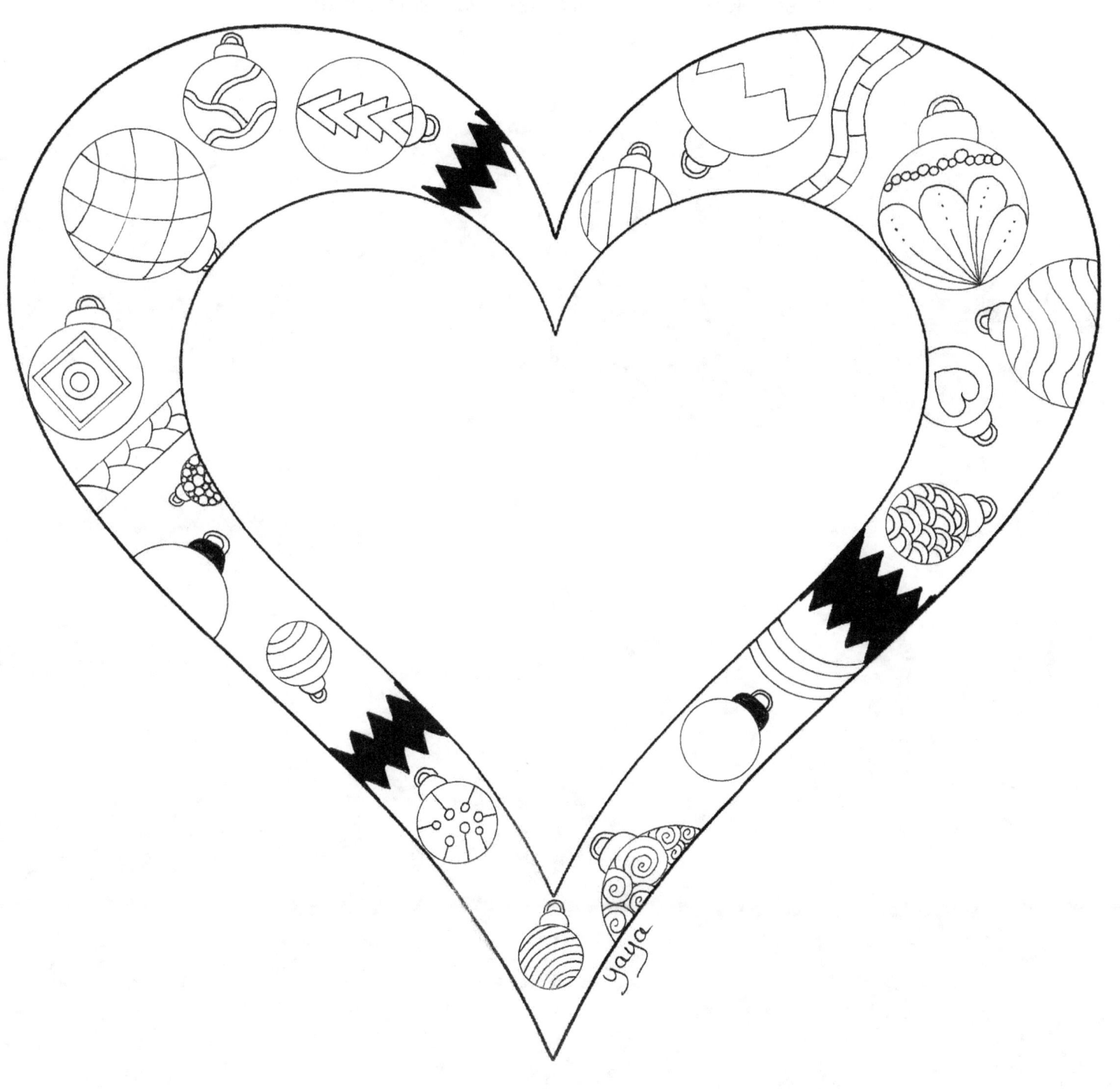

Contributing Artist
Yaya
France

Facebook : Les-gribouillis-de-yaya-georgia-merino

Contributing Artist
Yaya
France

Facebook : Les-gribouillis-de-yaya-georgia-merino

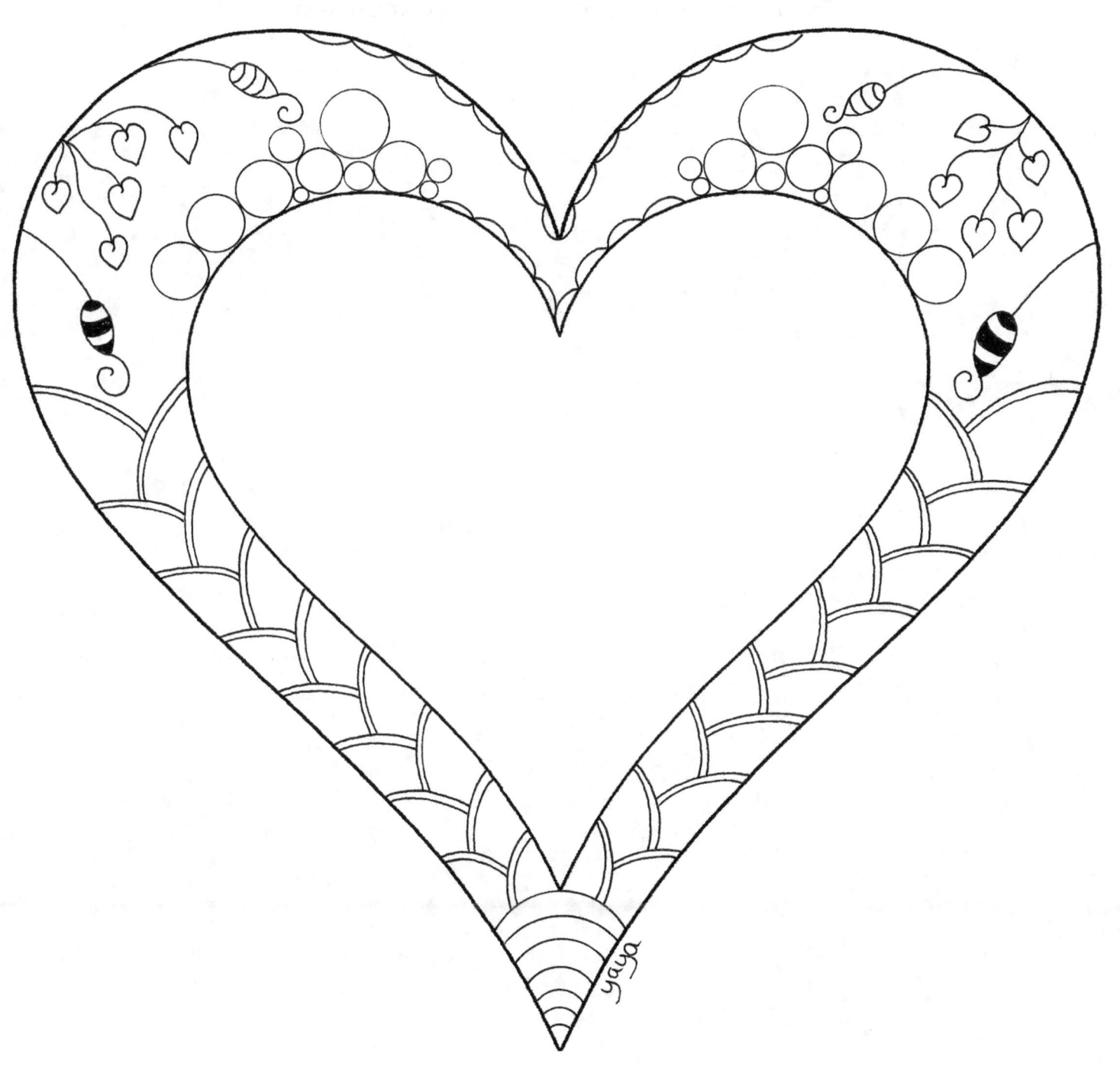

Contributing Artist
Yaya
France

Facebook : Les-gribouillis-de-yaya-georgia-merino

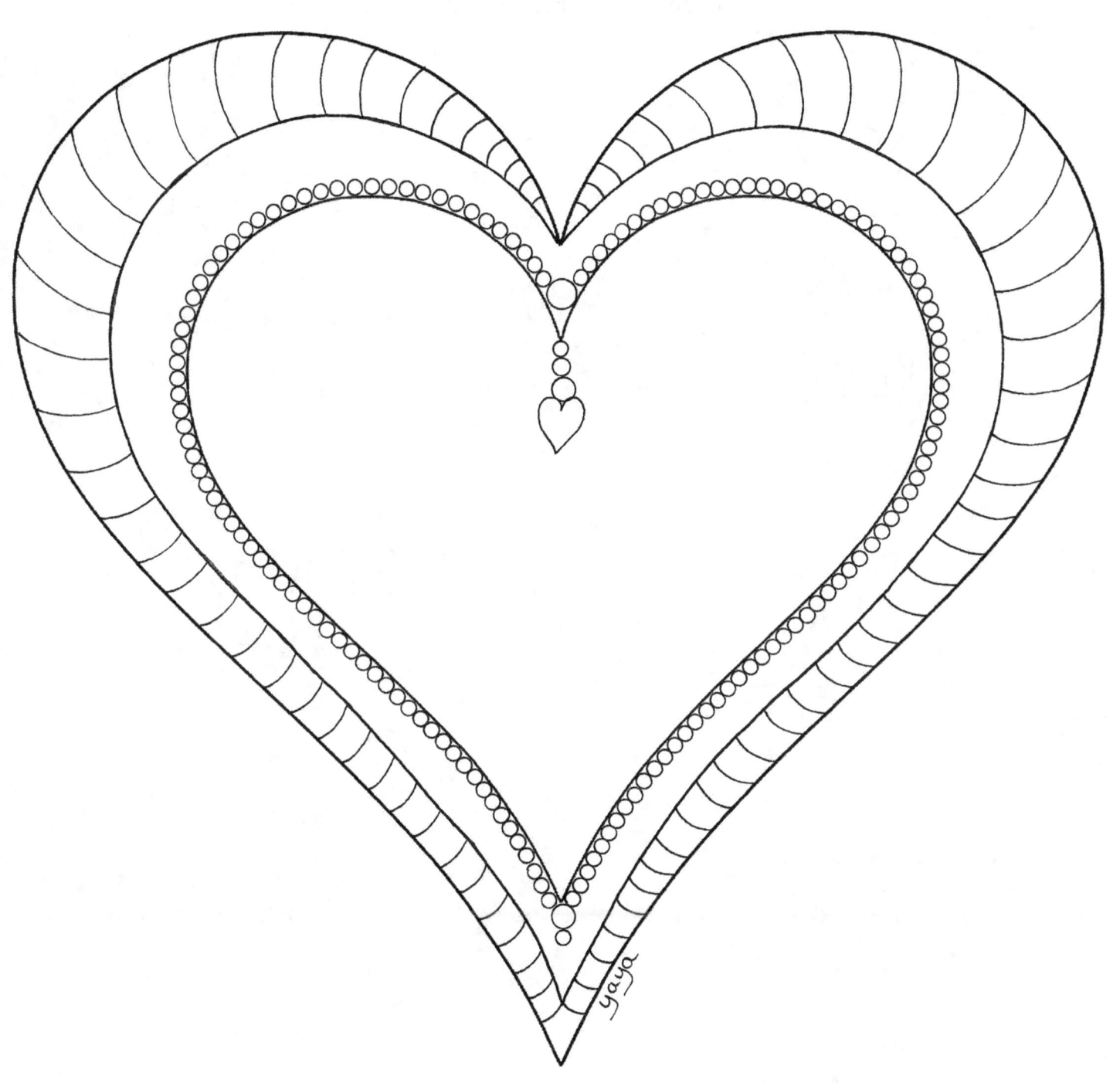

Contributing Artist
Arianne Schimmel
The Netherlands

Facebook : ArianneSchimmel

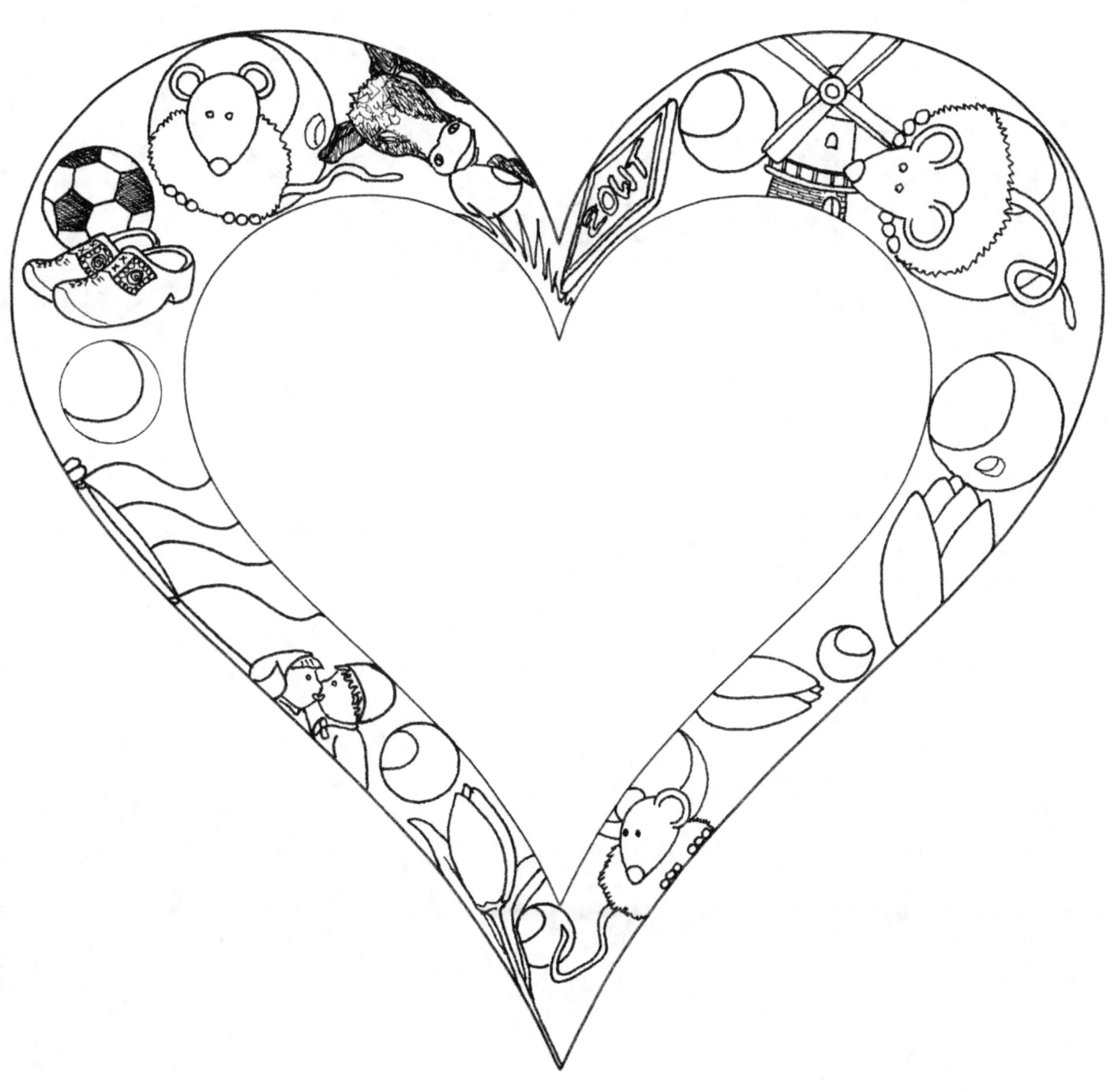

Contributing Artist
Arianne Schimmel
The Netherlands

Facebook : ArianneSchimmel

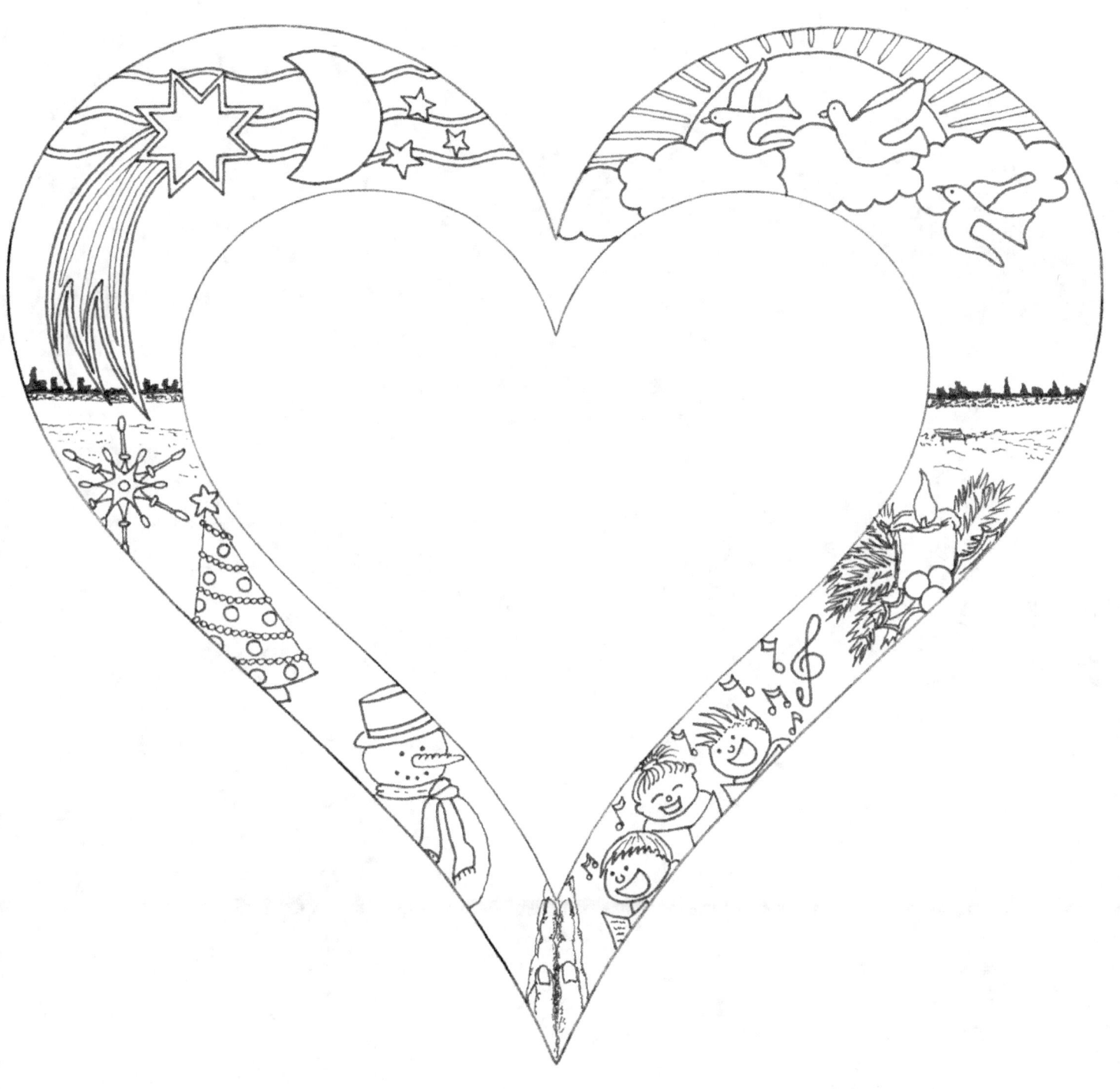

Contributing Artist
Alison Civil
UK

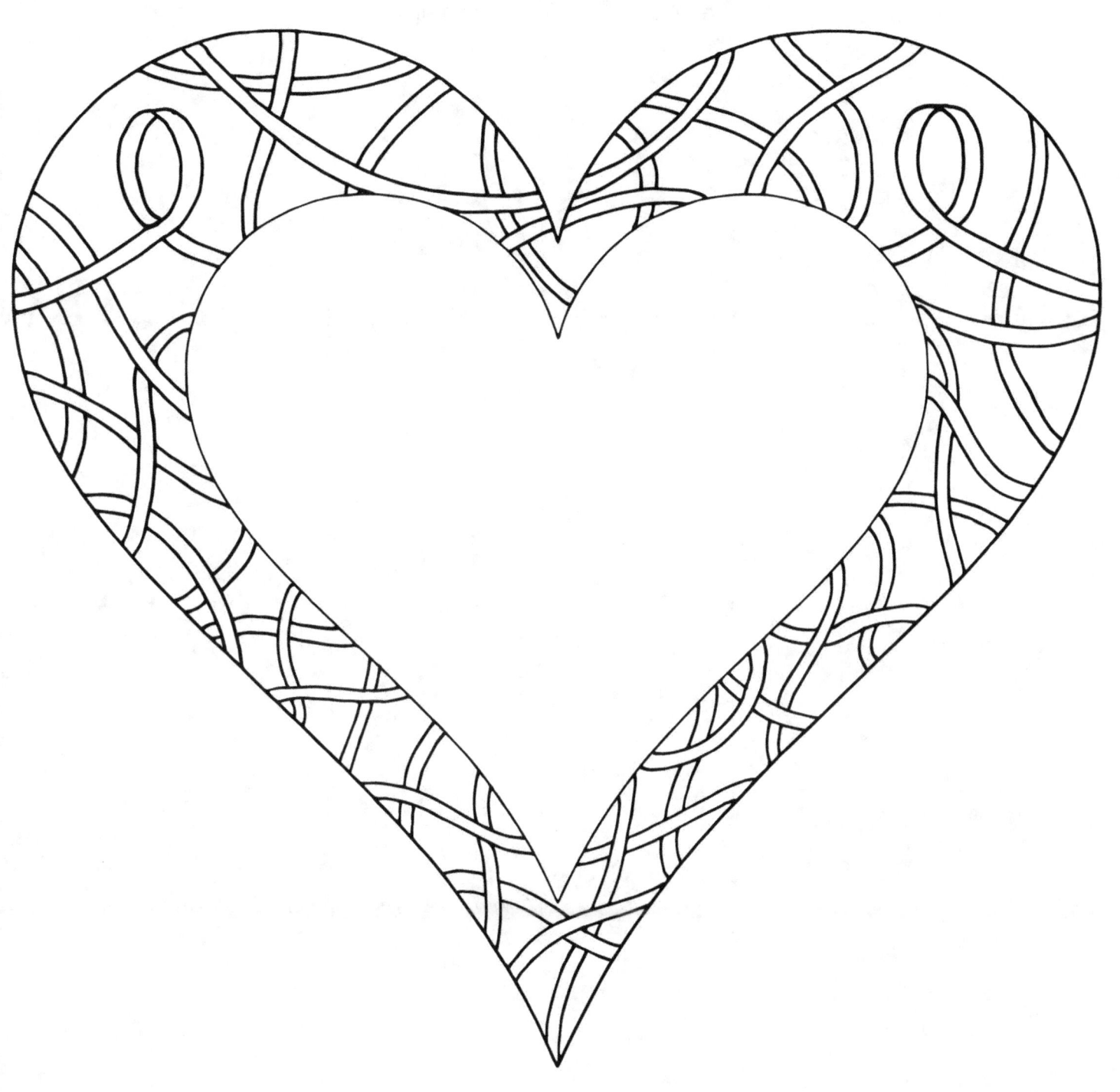

Contributing Artist
Alexius Hsing
Taiwan

Facebook : alexius.storry.teller

Contributing Artist
Alexius Hsing
Taiwan

Facebook : alexius.storry.teller

Contributing Artist
Alexius Hsing
Taiwan

Facebook : alexius.storry.teller

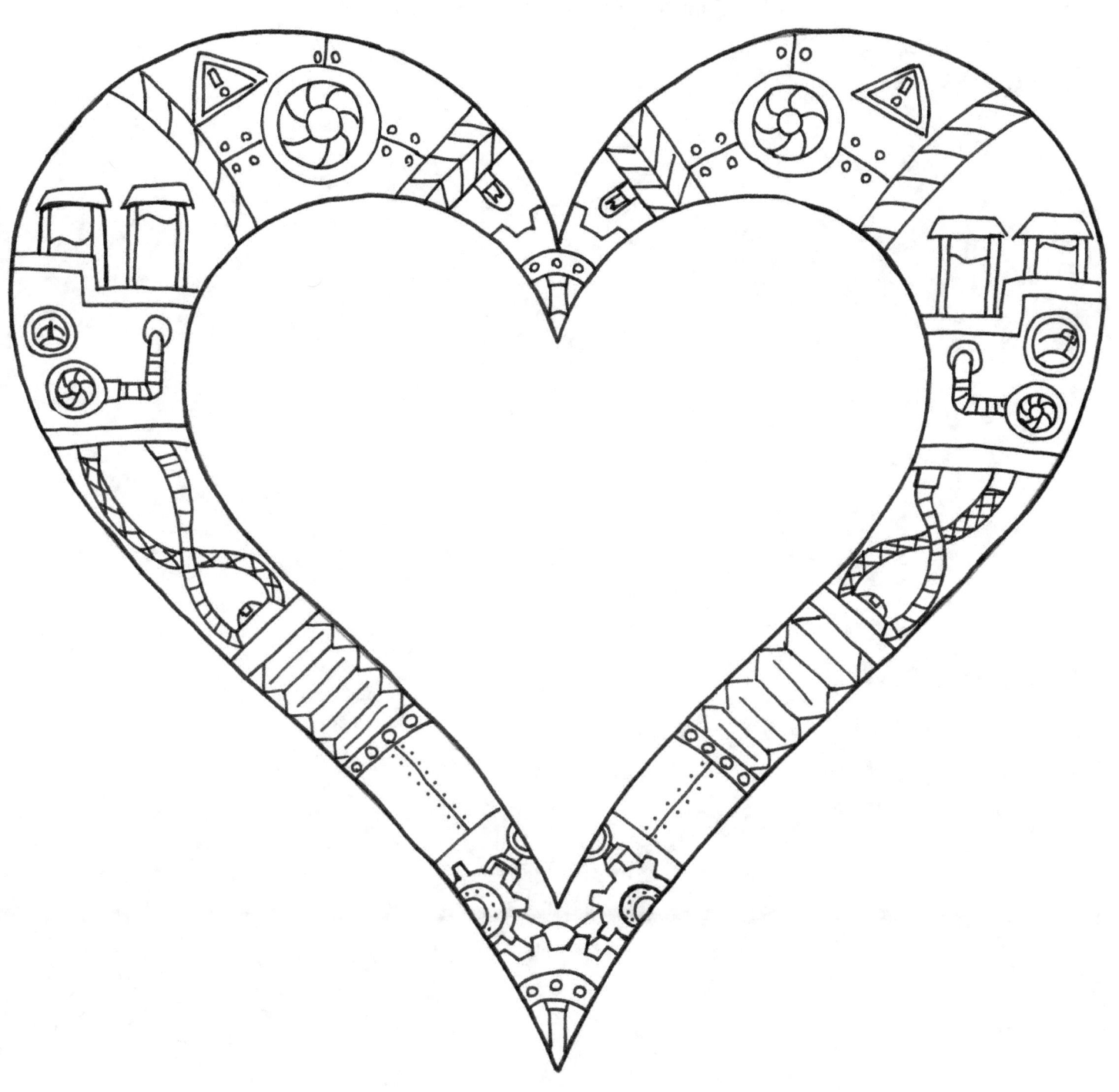

Contributing Artist
Alexius Hsing
Taiwan

Facebook : alexius.storry.teller

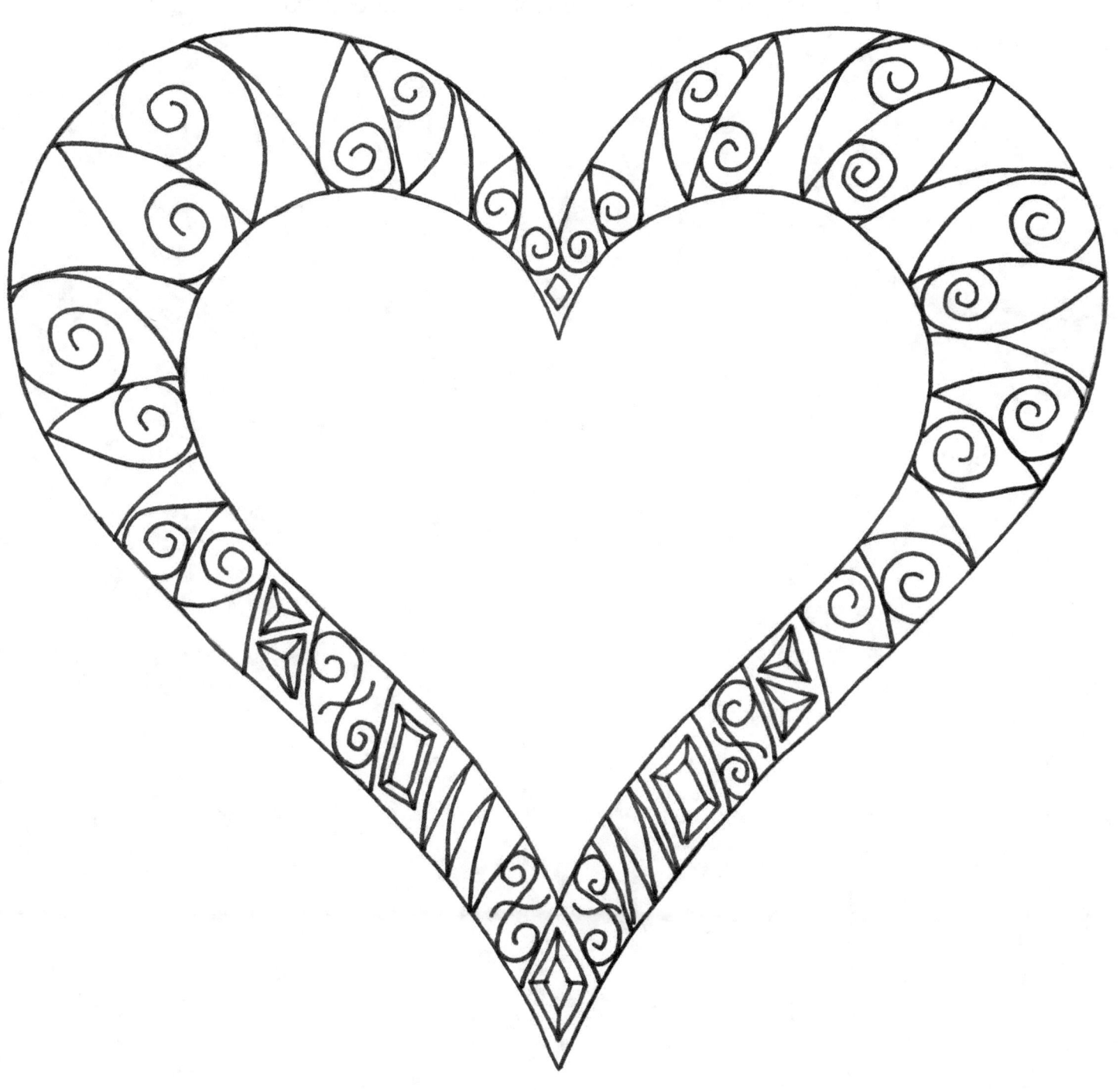

Contributing Artist
Amy Ke
Taiwan

Facebook : https://www.facebook.com/KA920000403000

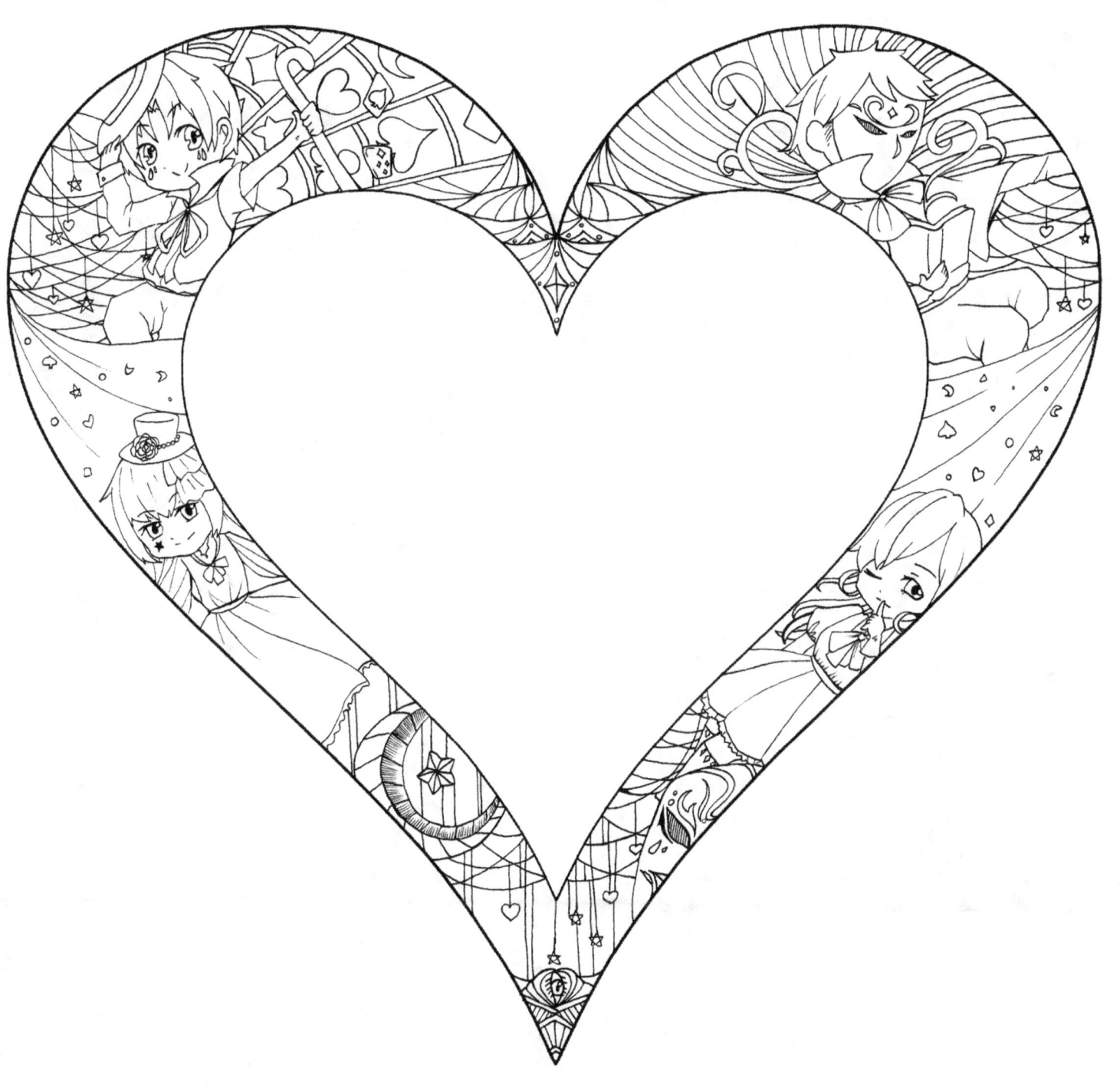

Contributing Artist
Angel Huang
Taiwan

Facebook : An99.Art

Contributing Artist
Debbie Lai
Taiwan

Facebook : DebbieDoodleGarden

Contributing Artist
Debbie Lai
Taiwan

Facebook : DebbieDoodleGarden

Contributing Artist
Debbie Lai
Taiwan

Facebook : DebbieDoodleGarden

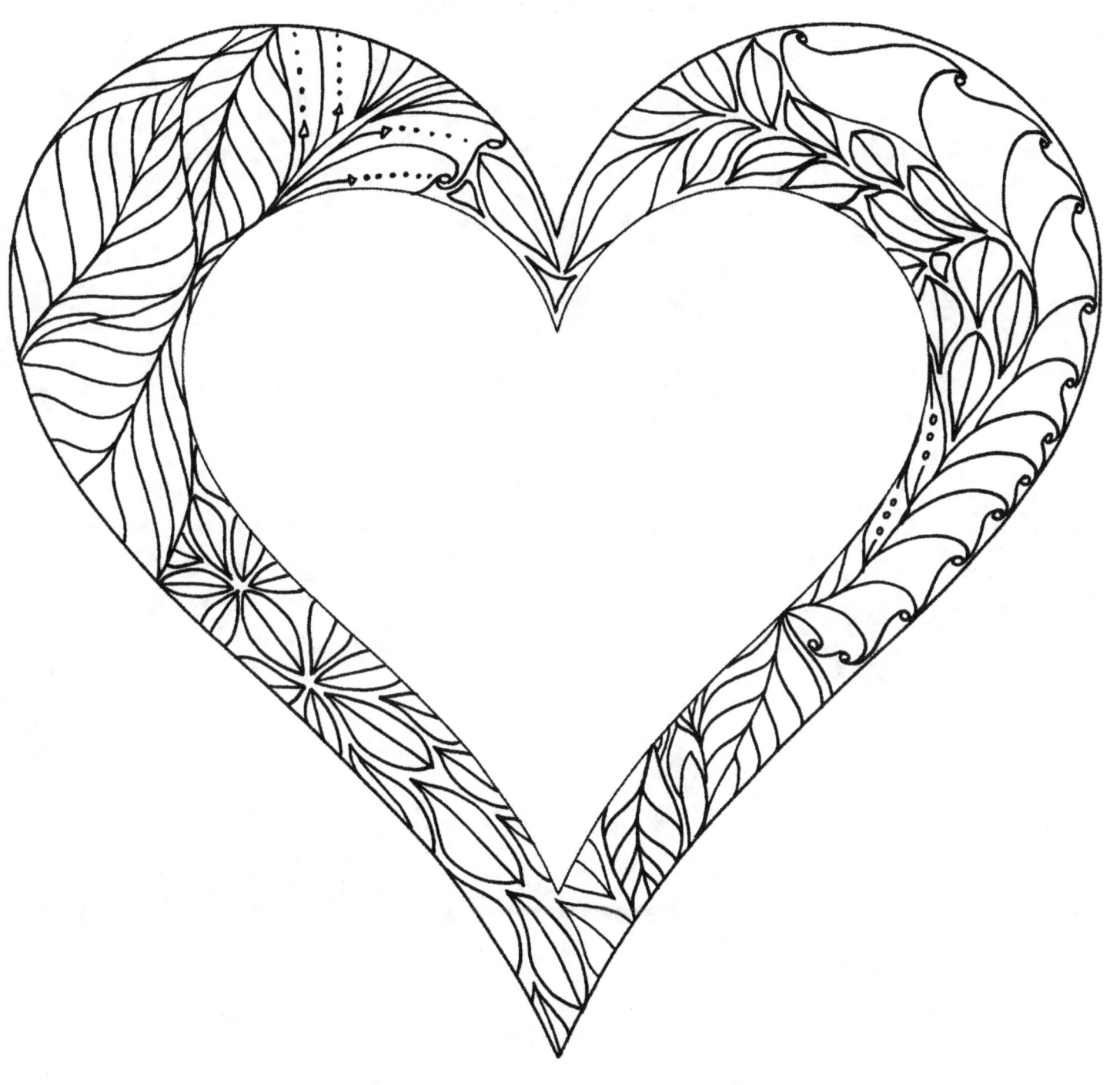

Contributing Artist
Hung Ai-Ling
Taiwan

Facebook : inspiredartLing

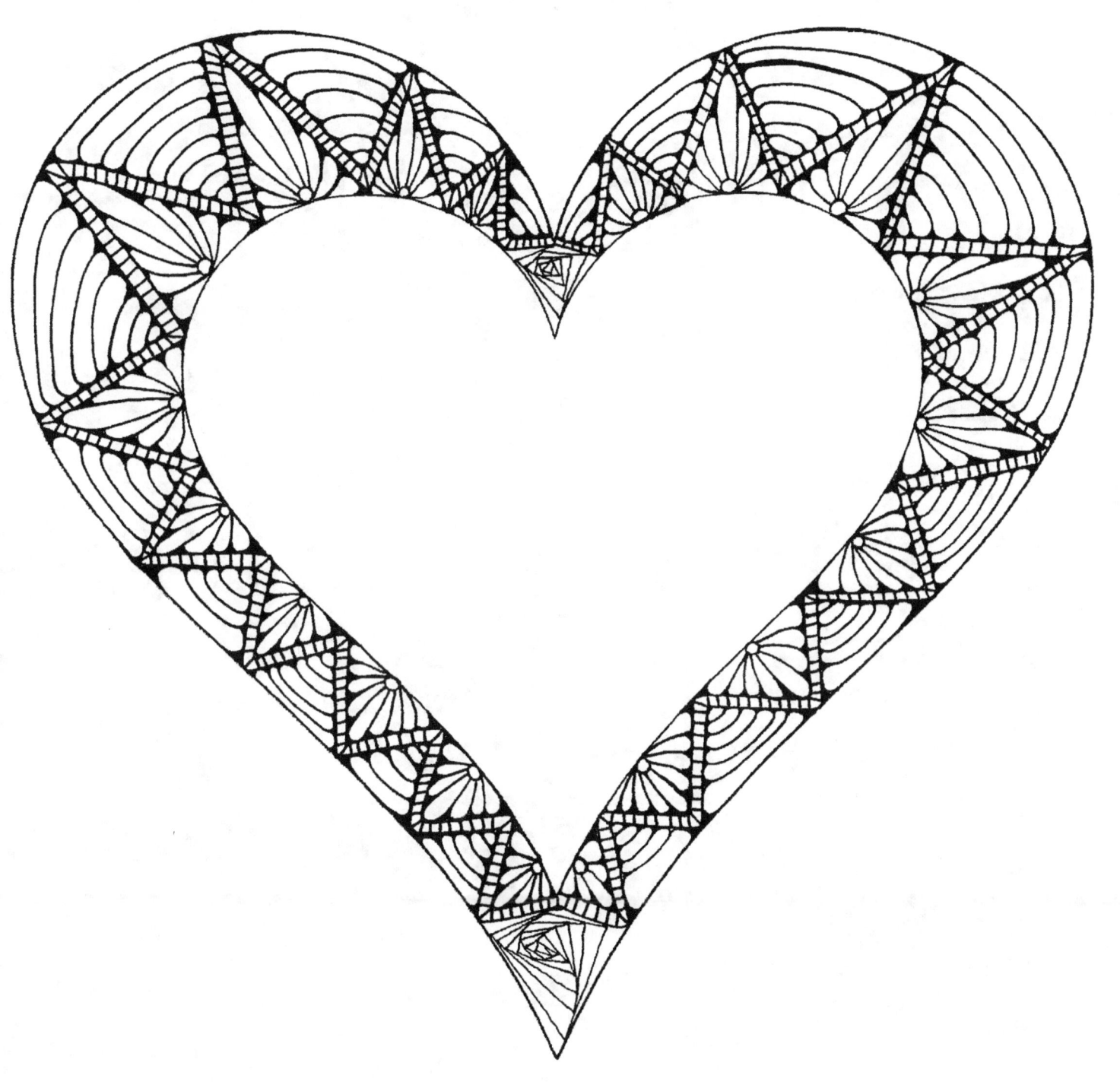

Contributing Artist
Jenny Wei
Taiwan

Facebook : zentanglefun

Contributing Artist
Jodi Ho
Taiwan

Facebook : riverho1688

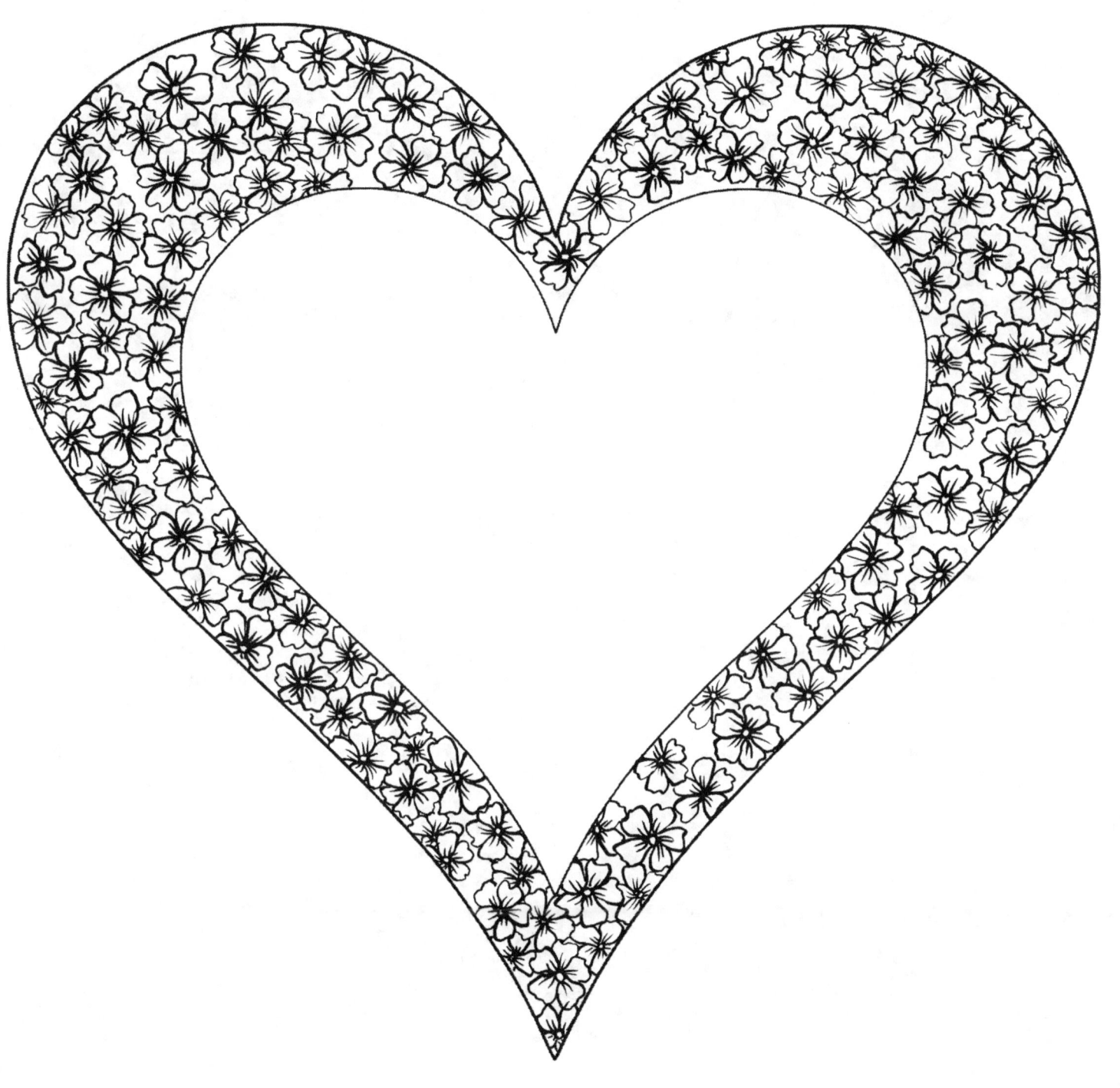

Contributing Artist
Jodi Ho
Taiwan

Facebook : riverho1688

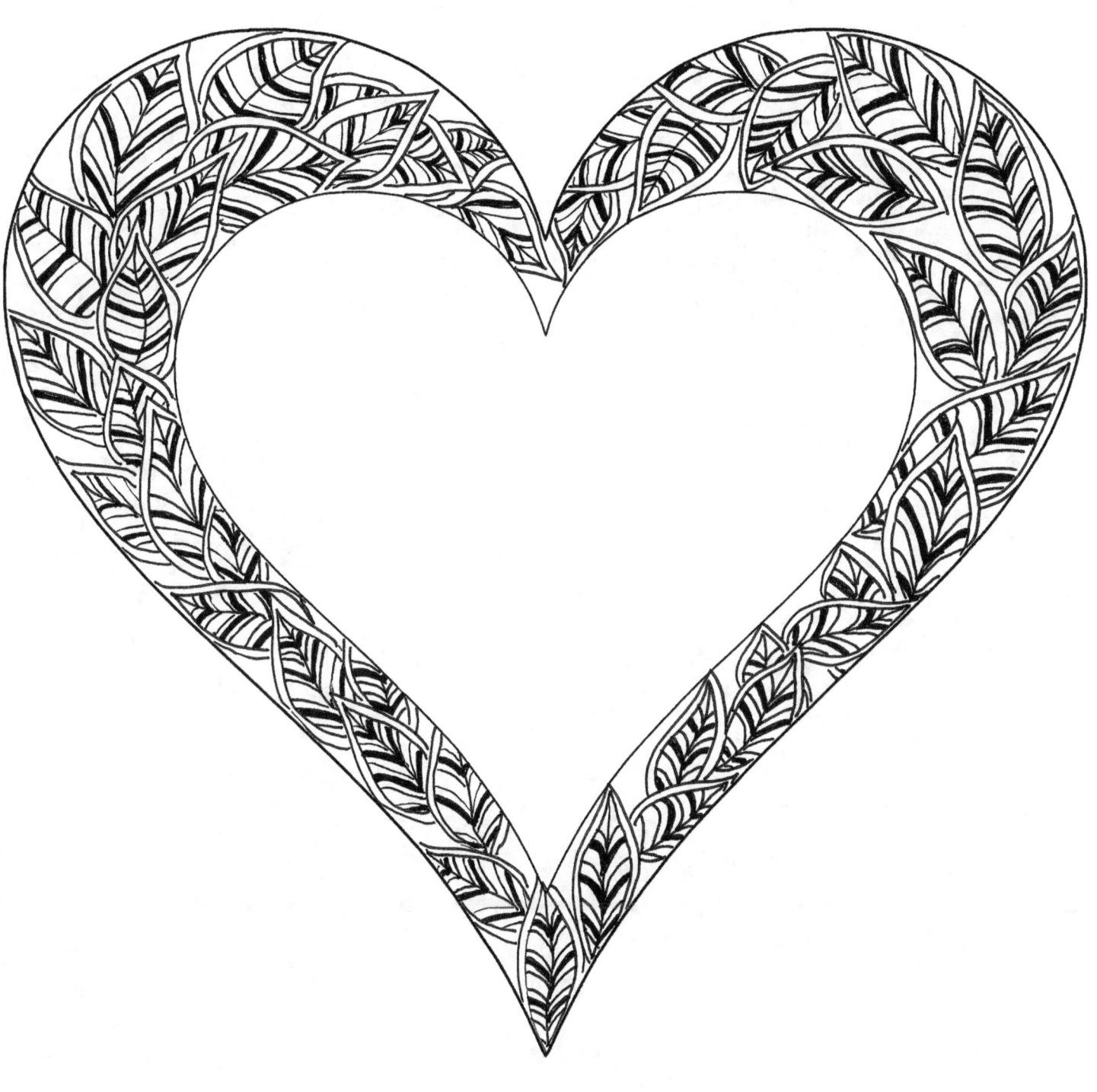

Contributing Artist
Jodi Ho
Taiwan

Facebook : riverho1688

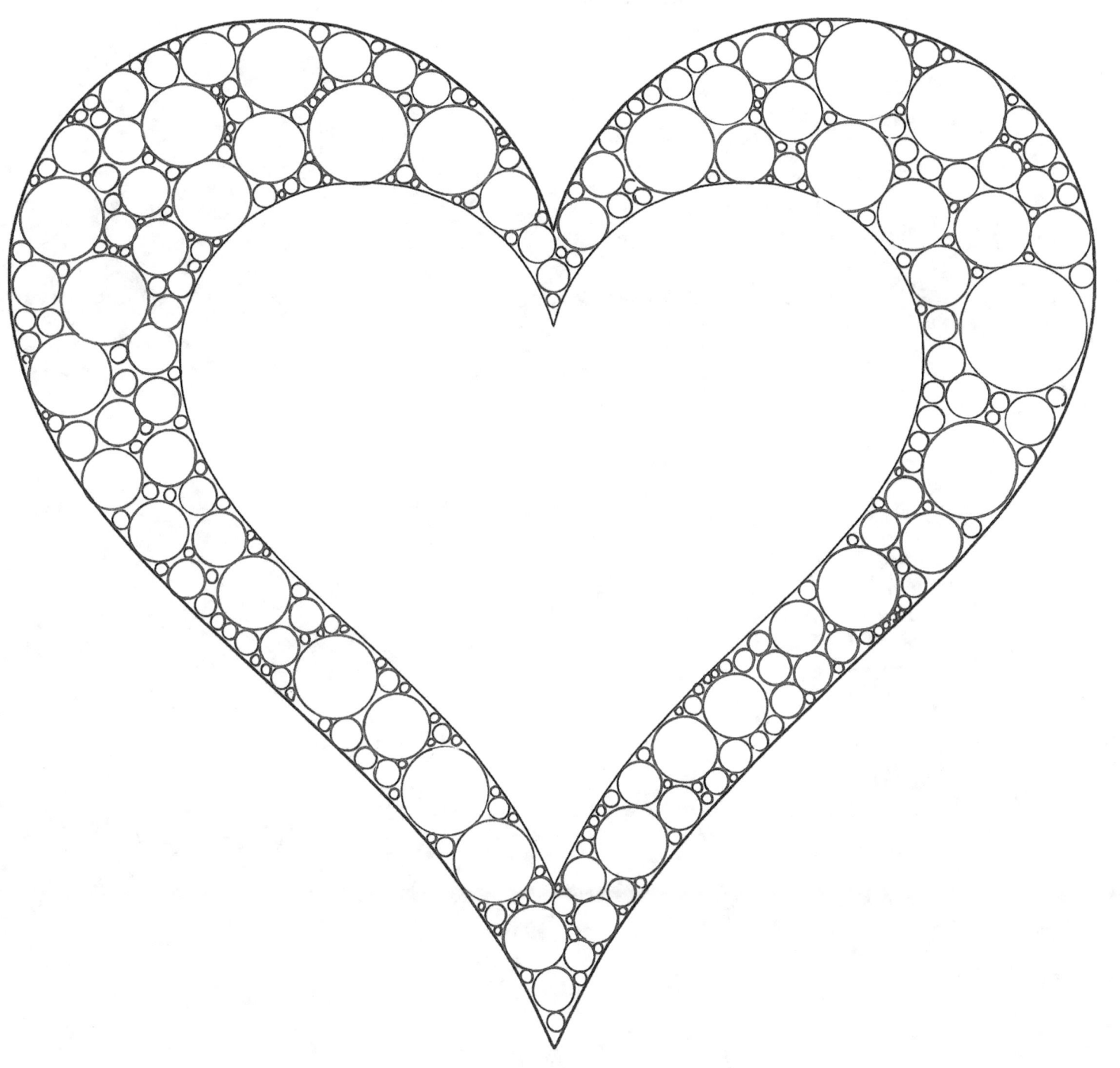

Contributing Artist
Jodi Ho
Taiwan

Facebook : riverho1688

Contributing Artist
Jodi Ho
Taiwan

Facebook : riverho1688

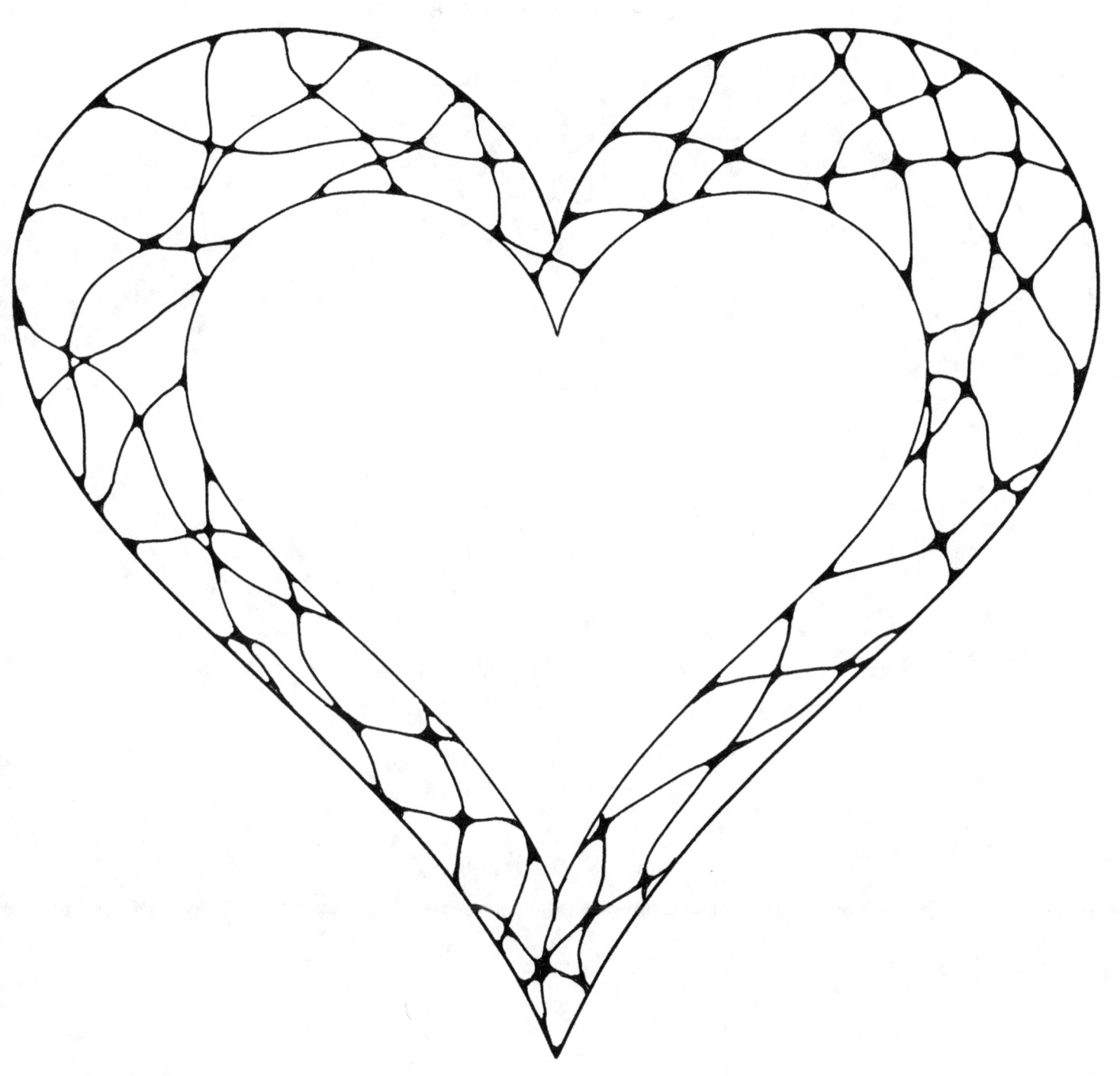

Contributing Artist
Jodi Ho
Taiwan

Facebook : riverho1688

Contributing Artist
Jovian Ke
Taiwan

Facebook : JK.Illustration

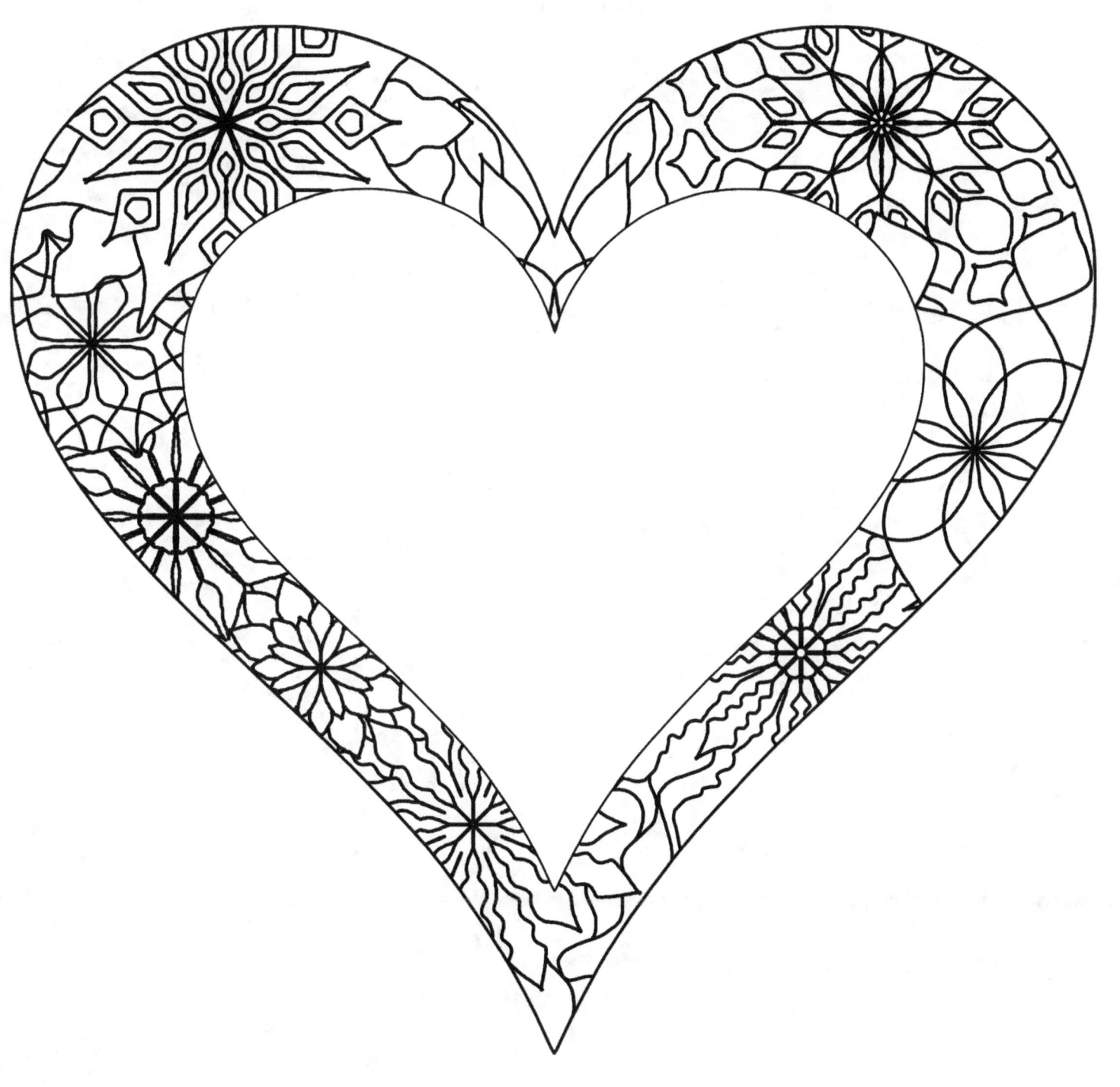

Contributing Artist
Leaf Yeh
Taiwan

Facebook : leaf.Painting

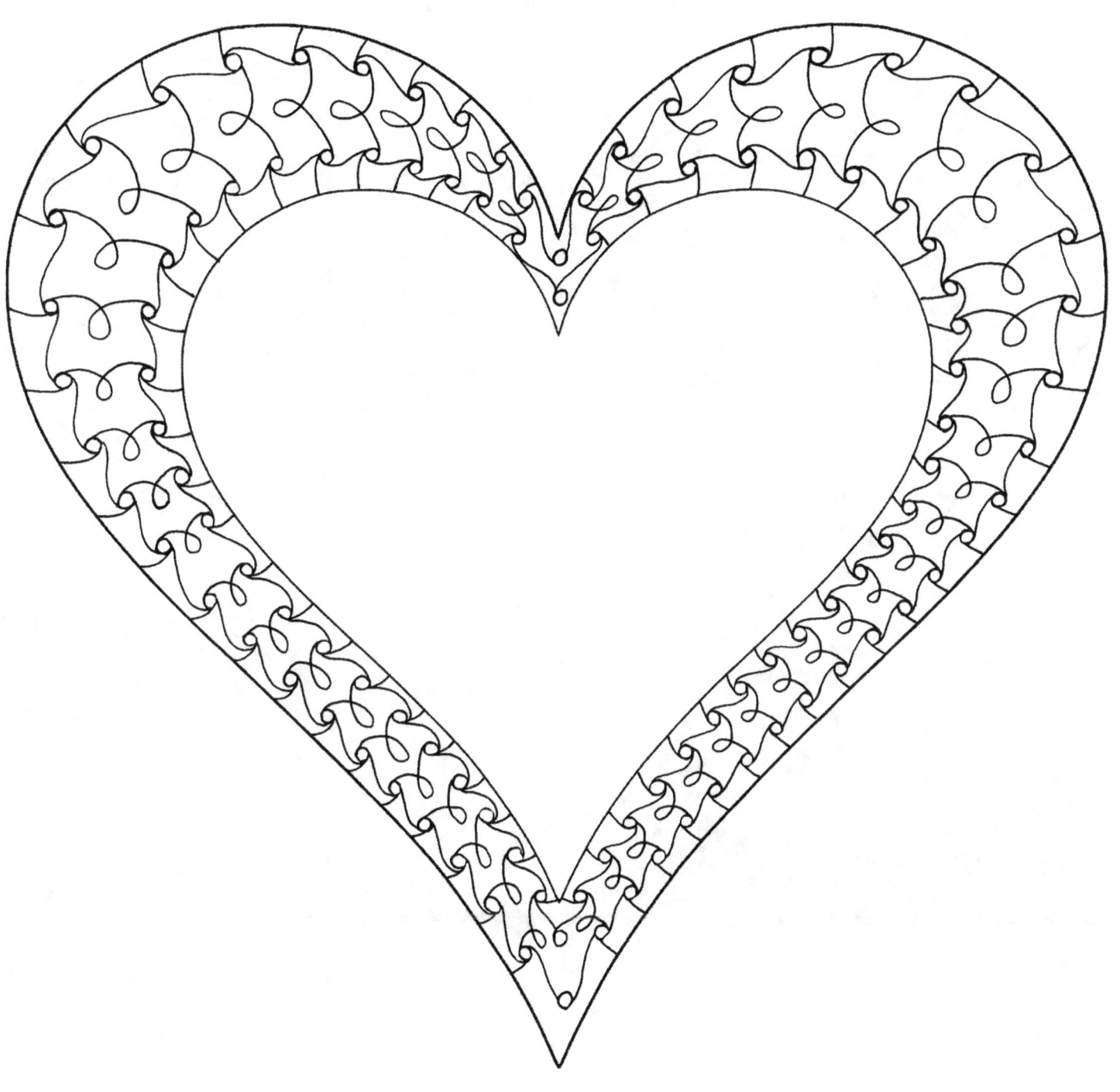

Contributing Artist
Leaf Yeh
Taiwan

Facebook : leaf.Painting

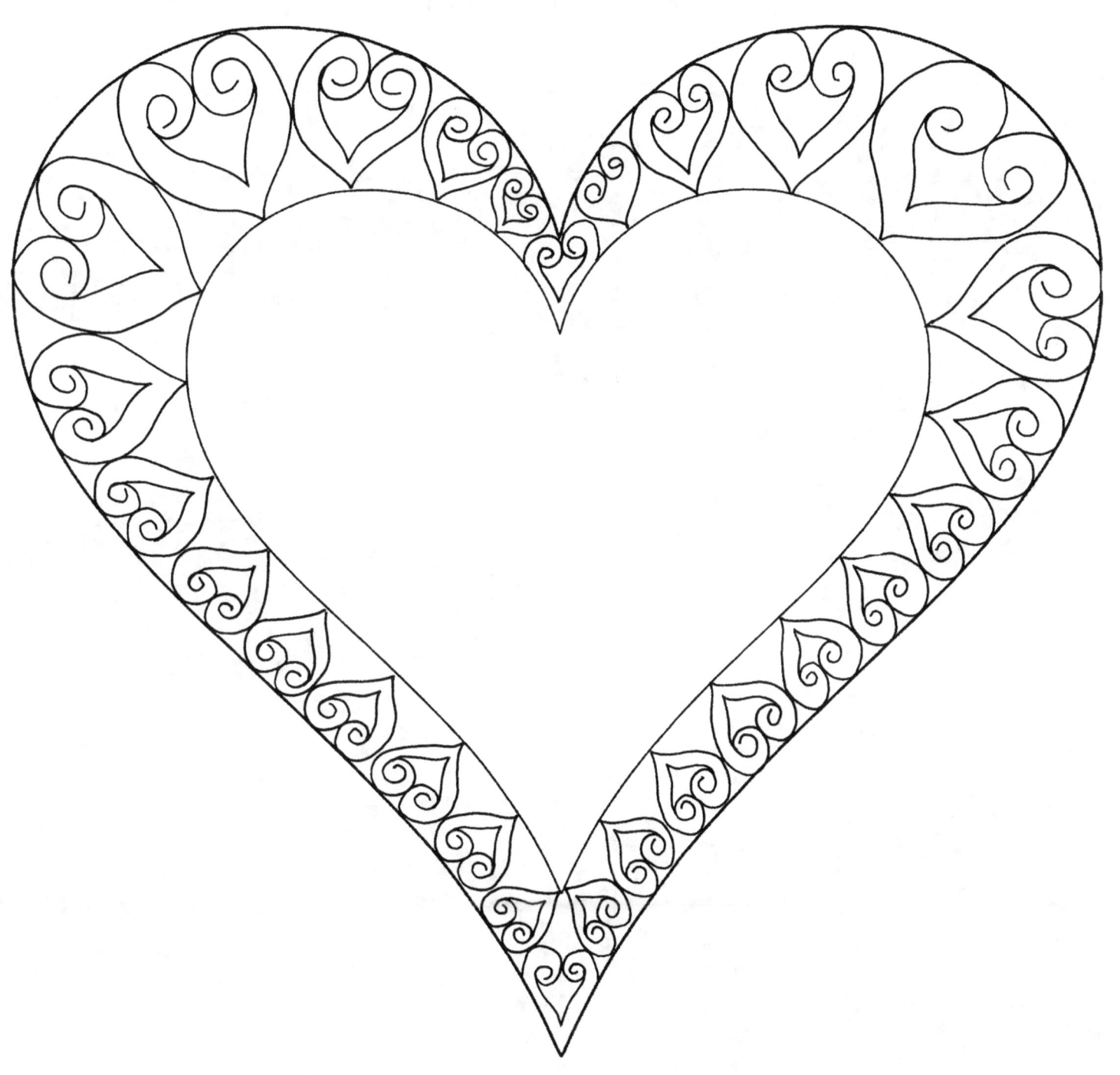

Contributing Artist
Leaf Yeh
Taiwan

Facebook : leaf.Painting

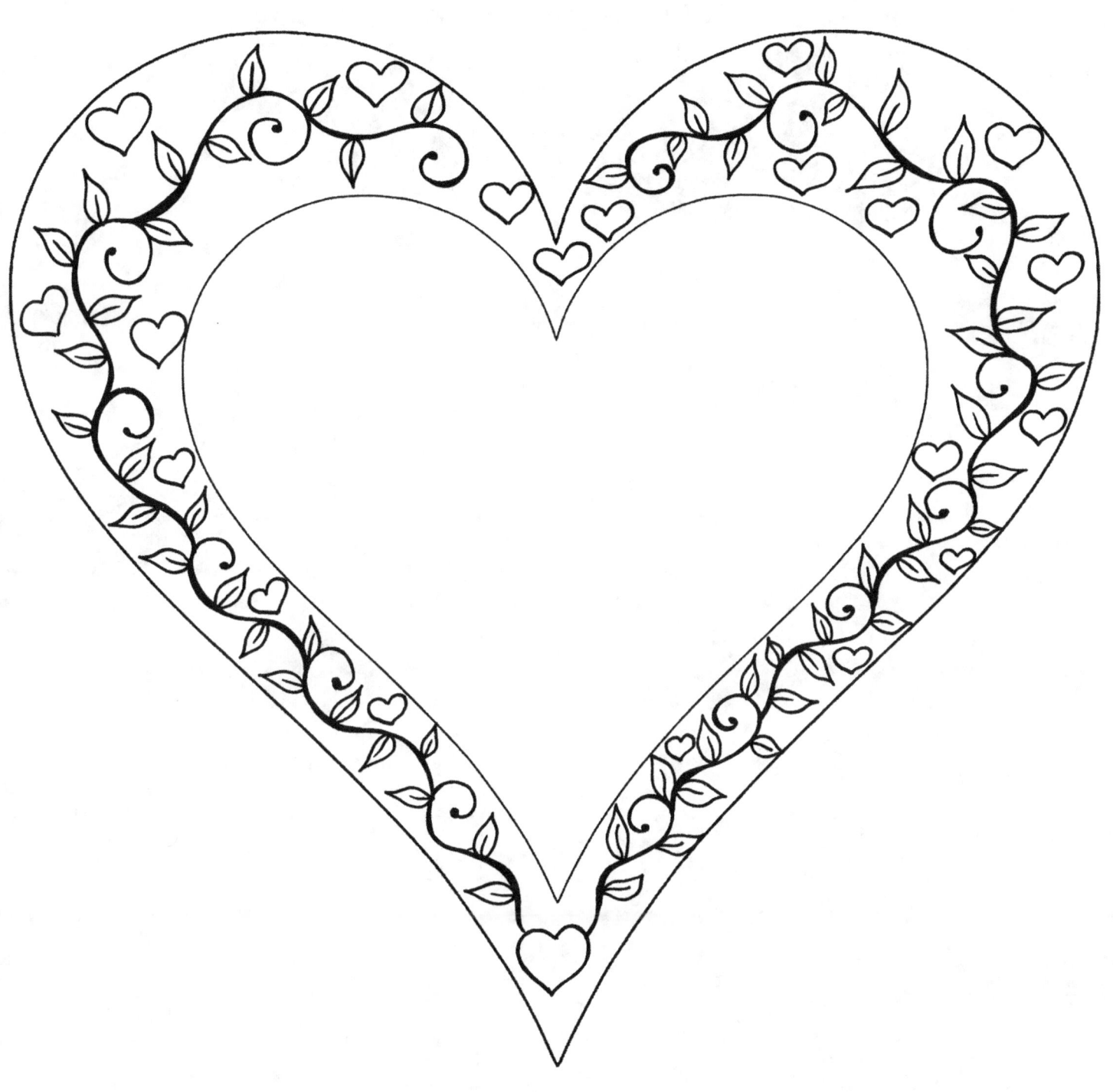

Contributing Artist
Leaf Yeh
Taiwan

Facebook : leaf.Painting

Contributing Artist
Leaf Yeh
Taiwan

Facebook : leaf.Painting

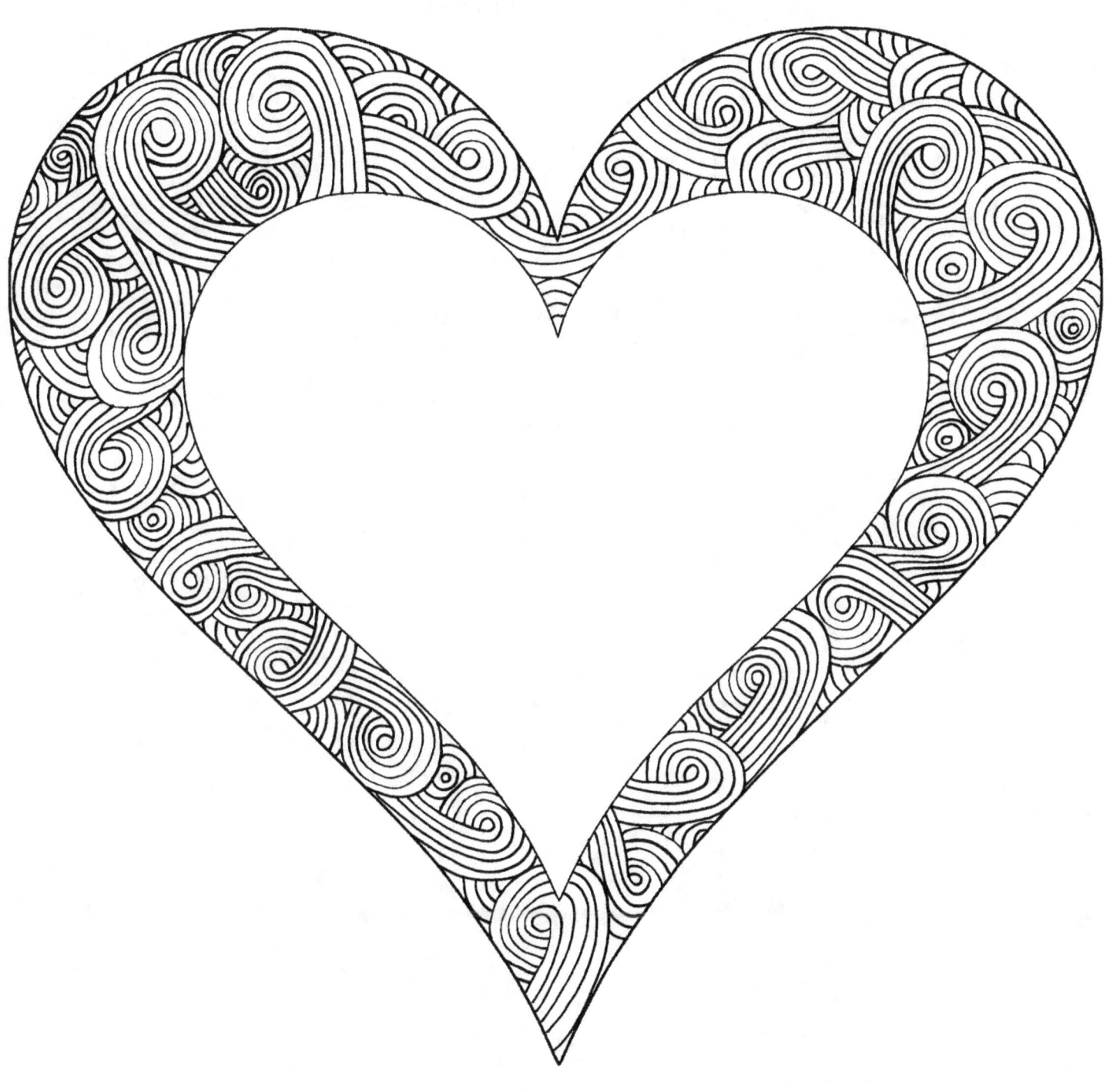

Contributing Artist
Leaf Yeh
Taiwan

Facebook : leaf.Painting

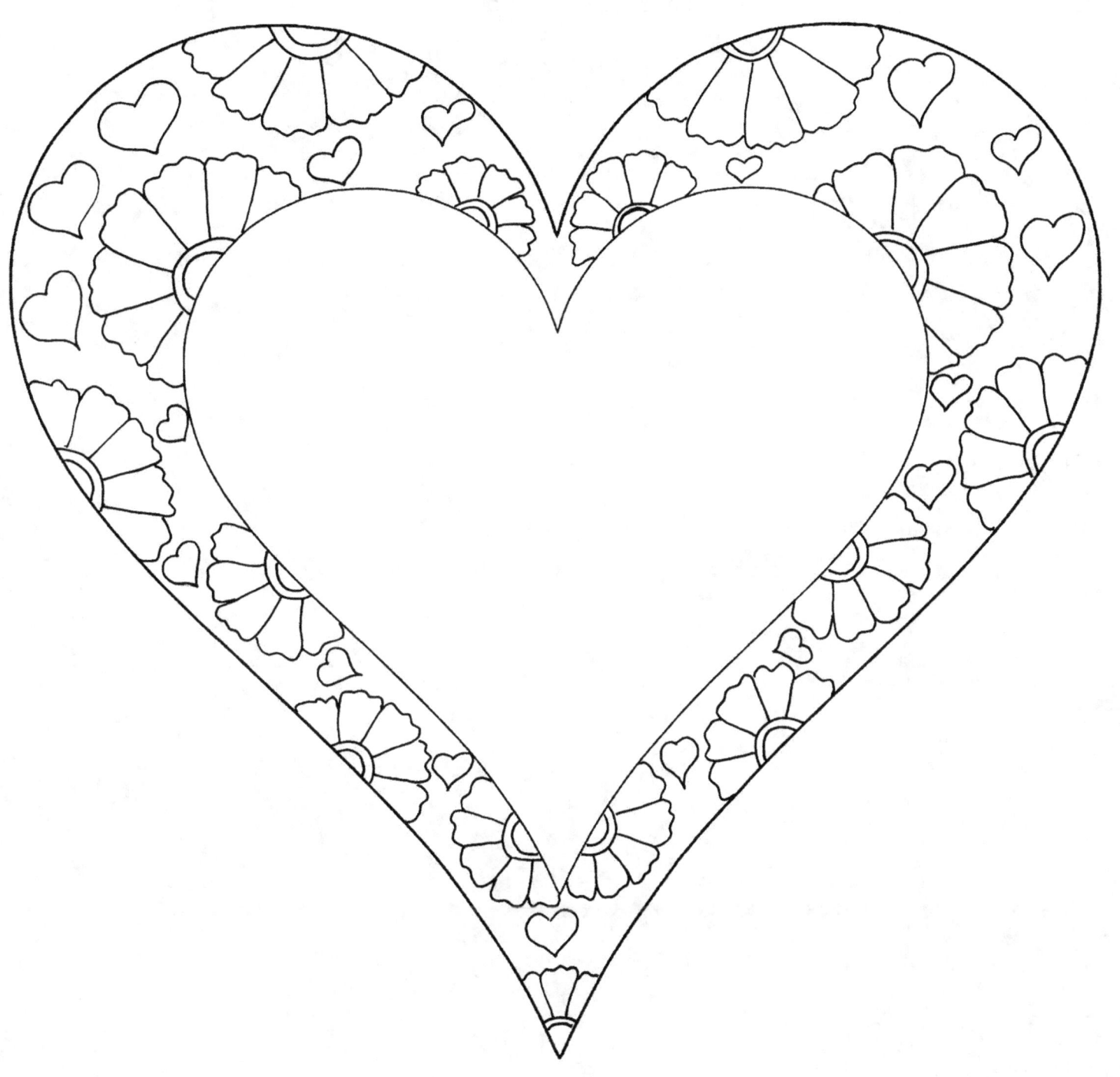

Contributing Artist
Leaf Yeh
Taiwan

Facebook : leaf.Painting

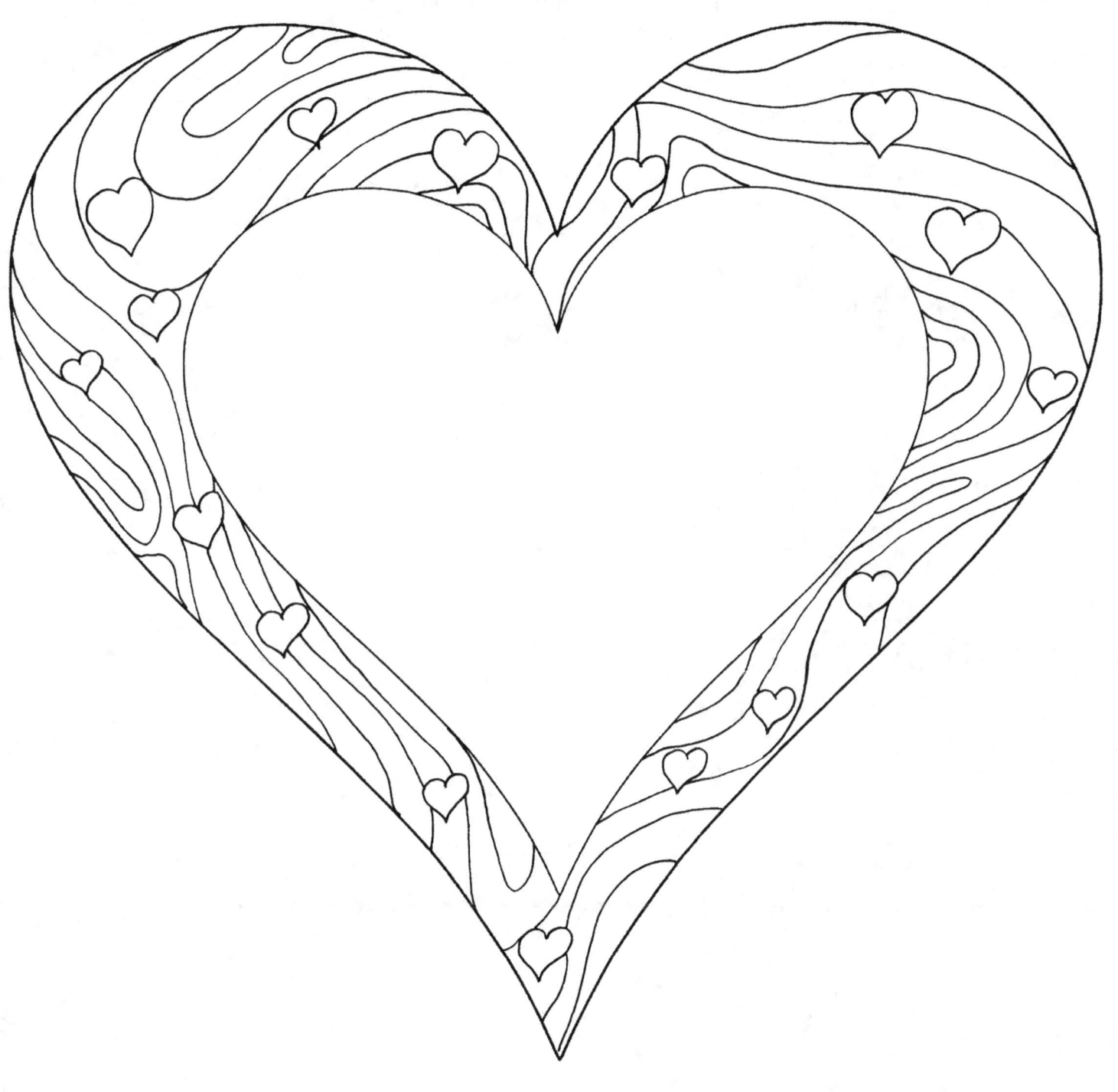

Contributing Artist
Lin Chiu
Taiwan

Facebook : ZentangleArt0626
Website : http://czt17lin.tumblr.com/

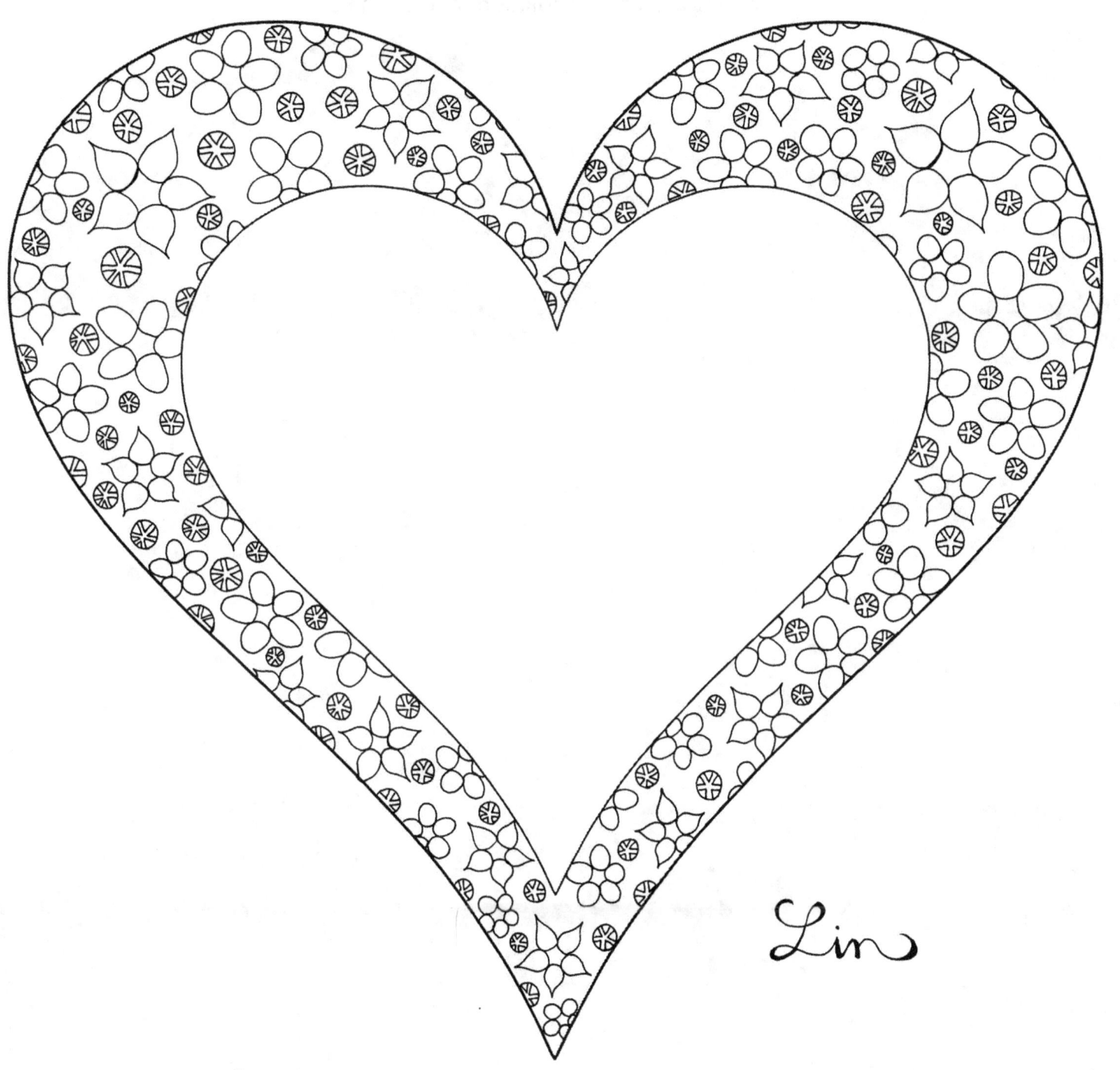

Contributing Artist
Mina Hsiao
Taiwan

https://www.facebook.com/czt19mina

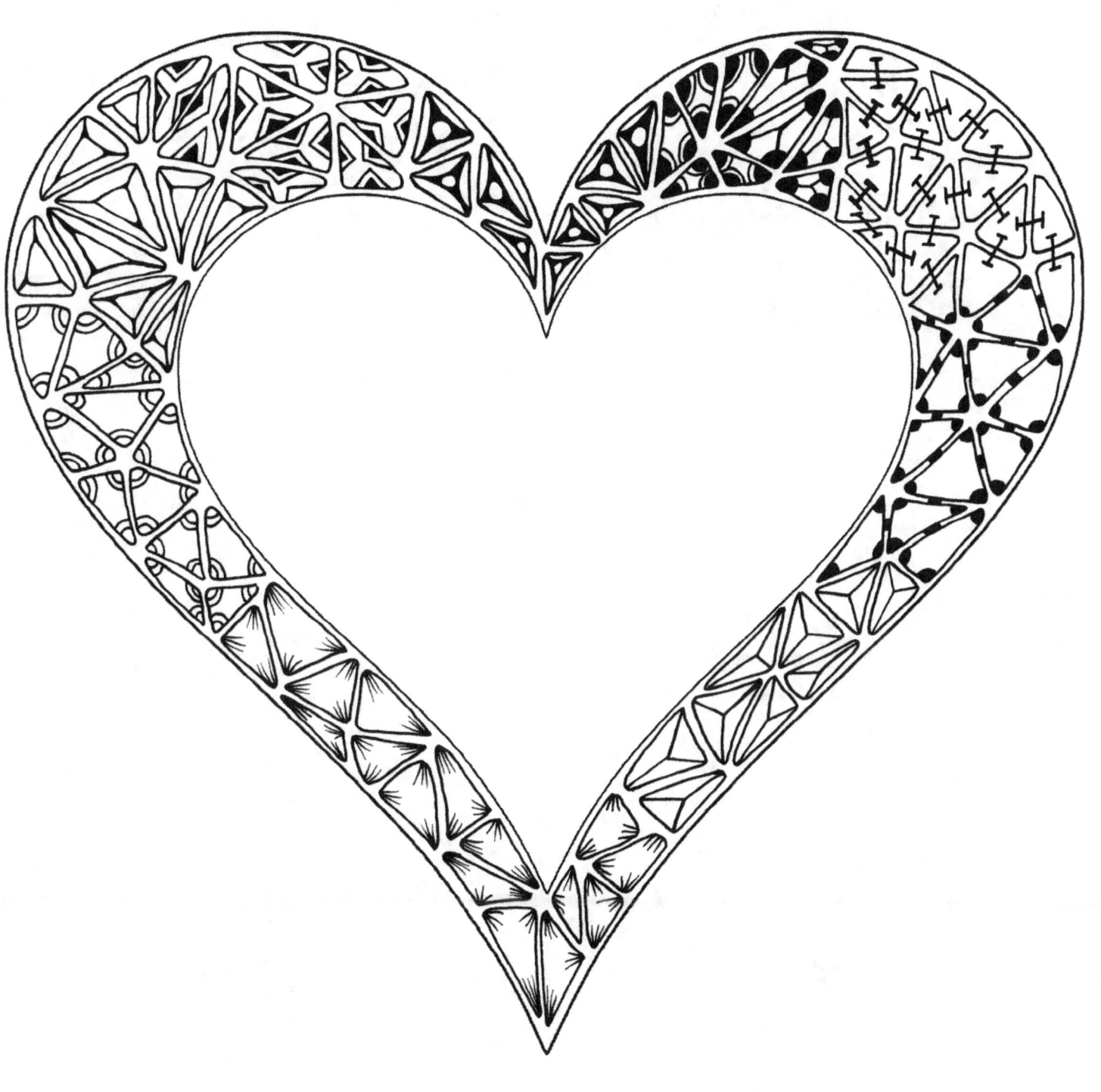

Contributing Artist
Mina Hsiao
Taiwan

https://www.facebook.com/czt19mina

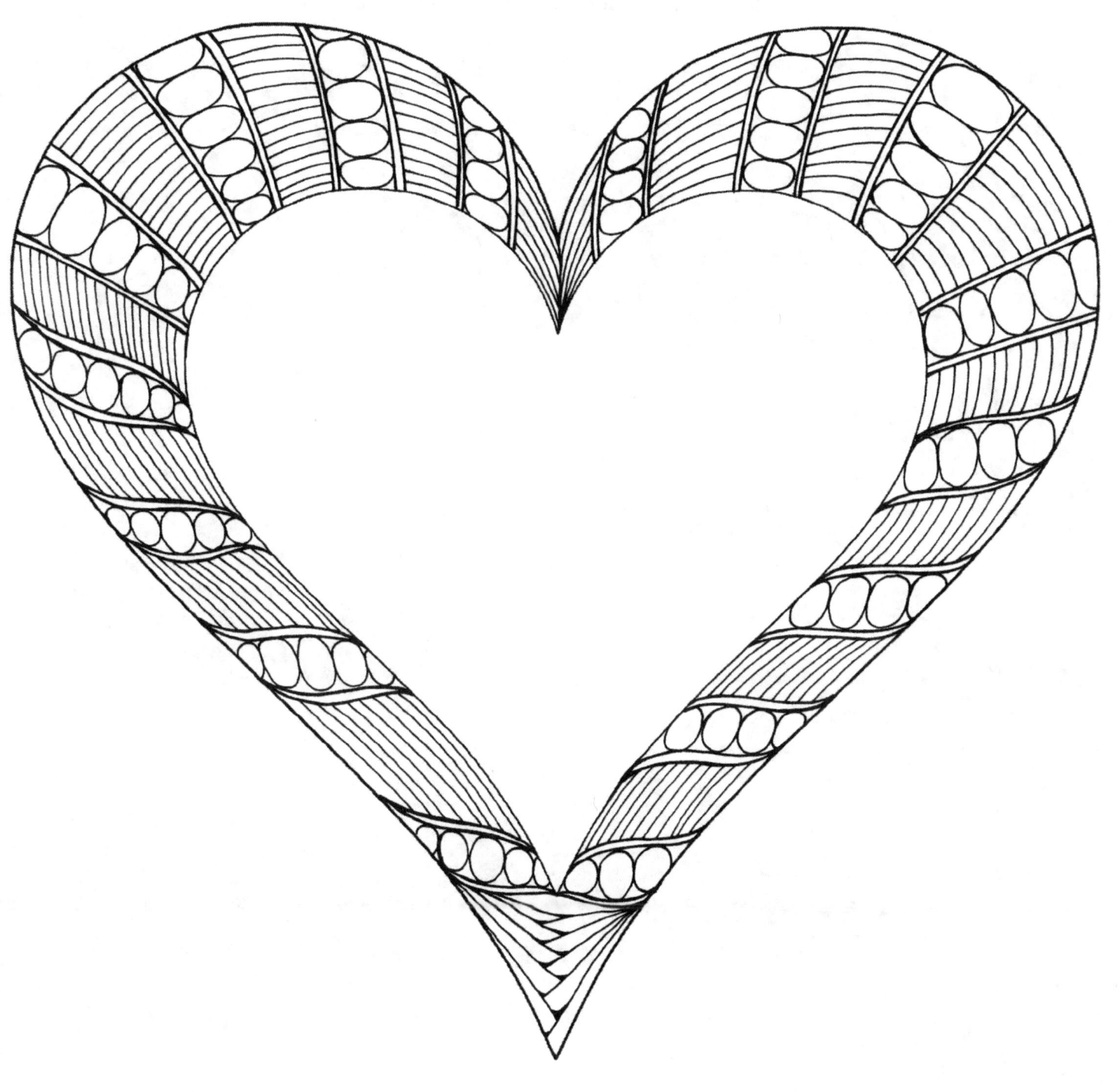

Contributing Artist
Mina Hsiao
Taiwan

https://www.facebook.com/czt19mina

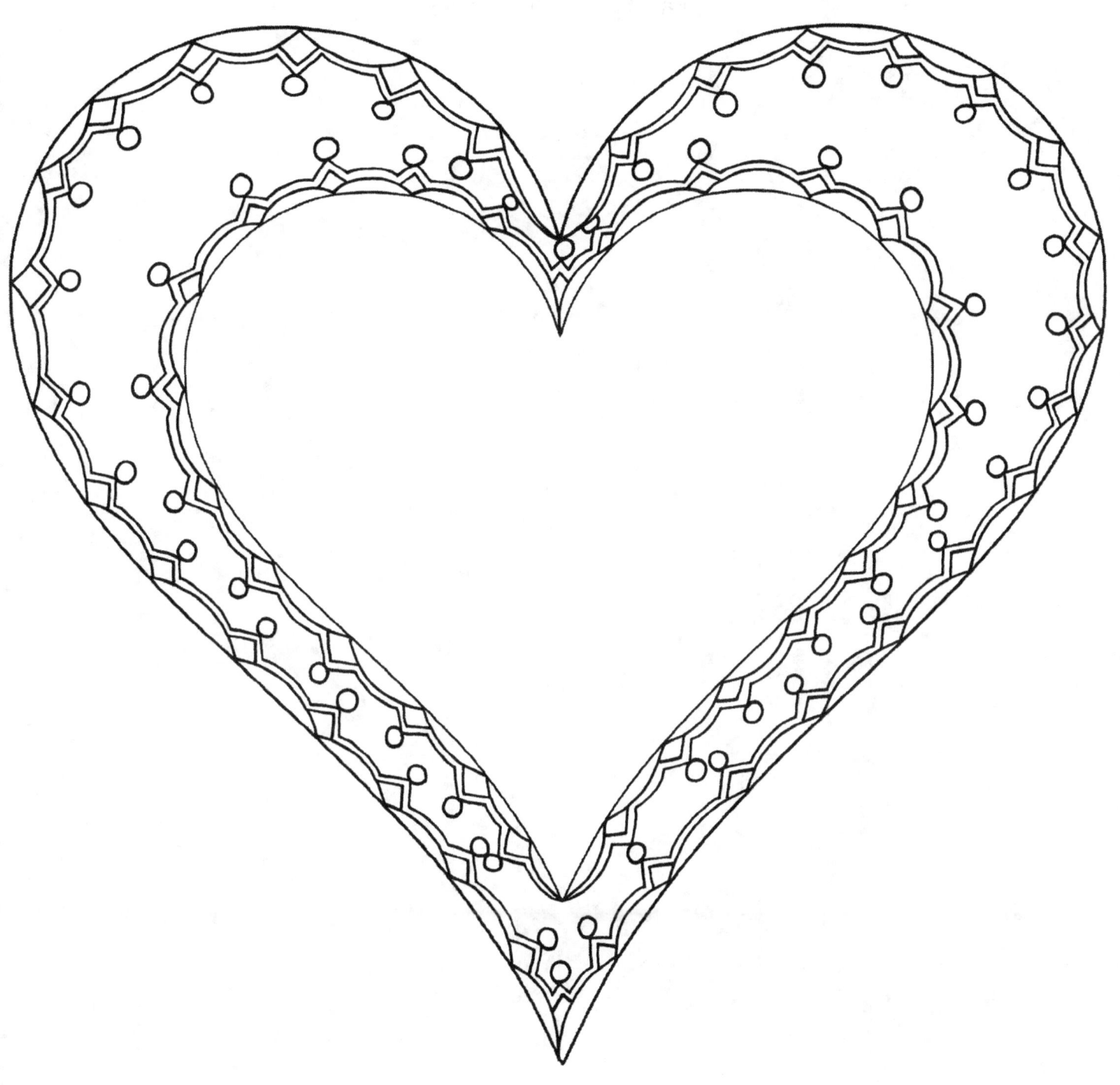

Contributing Artist
Nancy Liu
Taiwan

Facebook : 43Nancy43

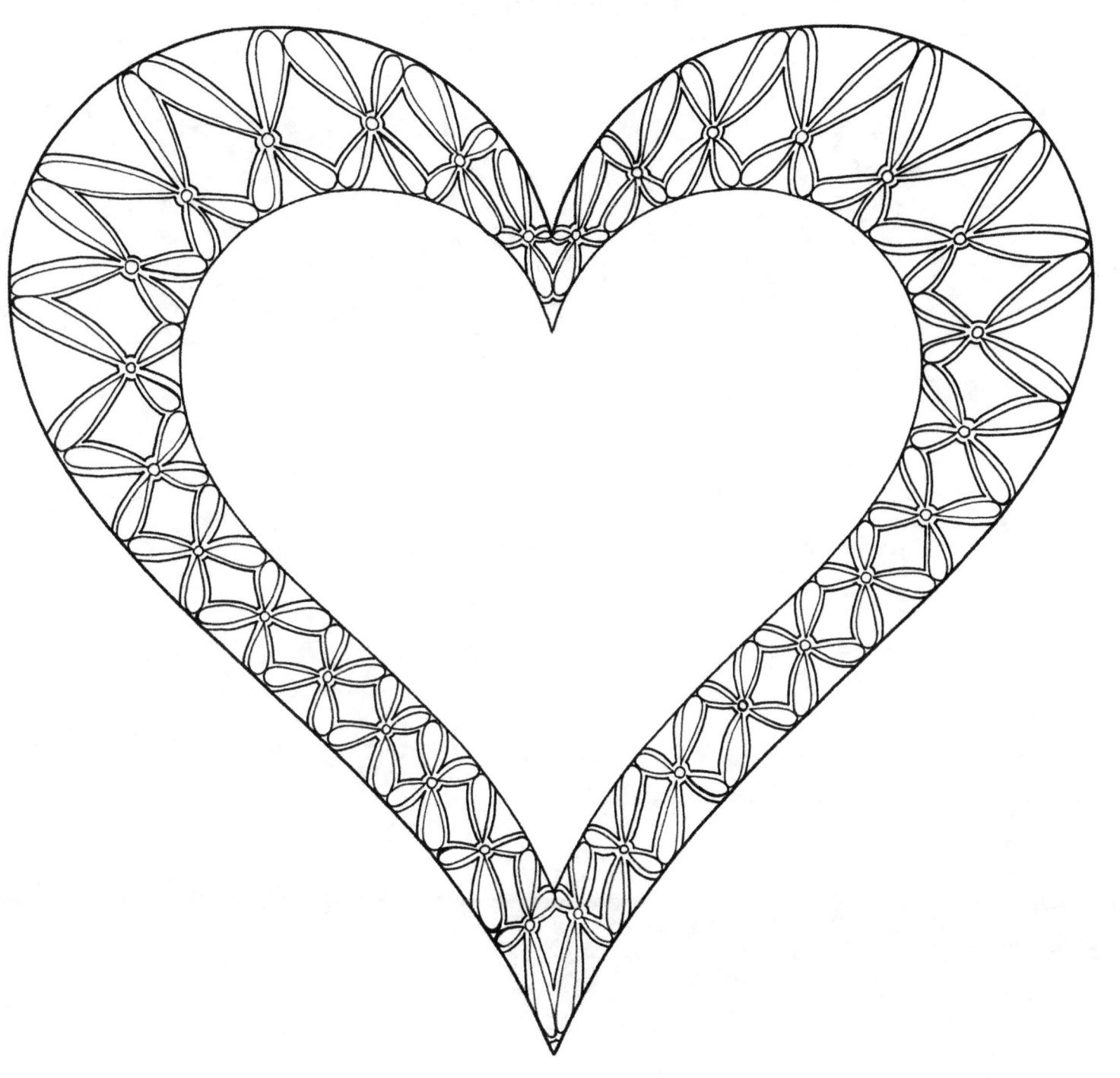

Contributing Artist
Nancy Liu
Taiwan

Facebook : 43Nancy43

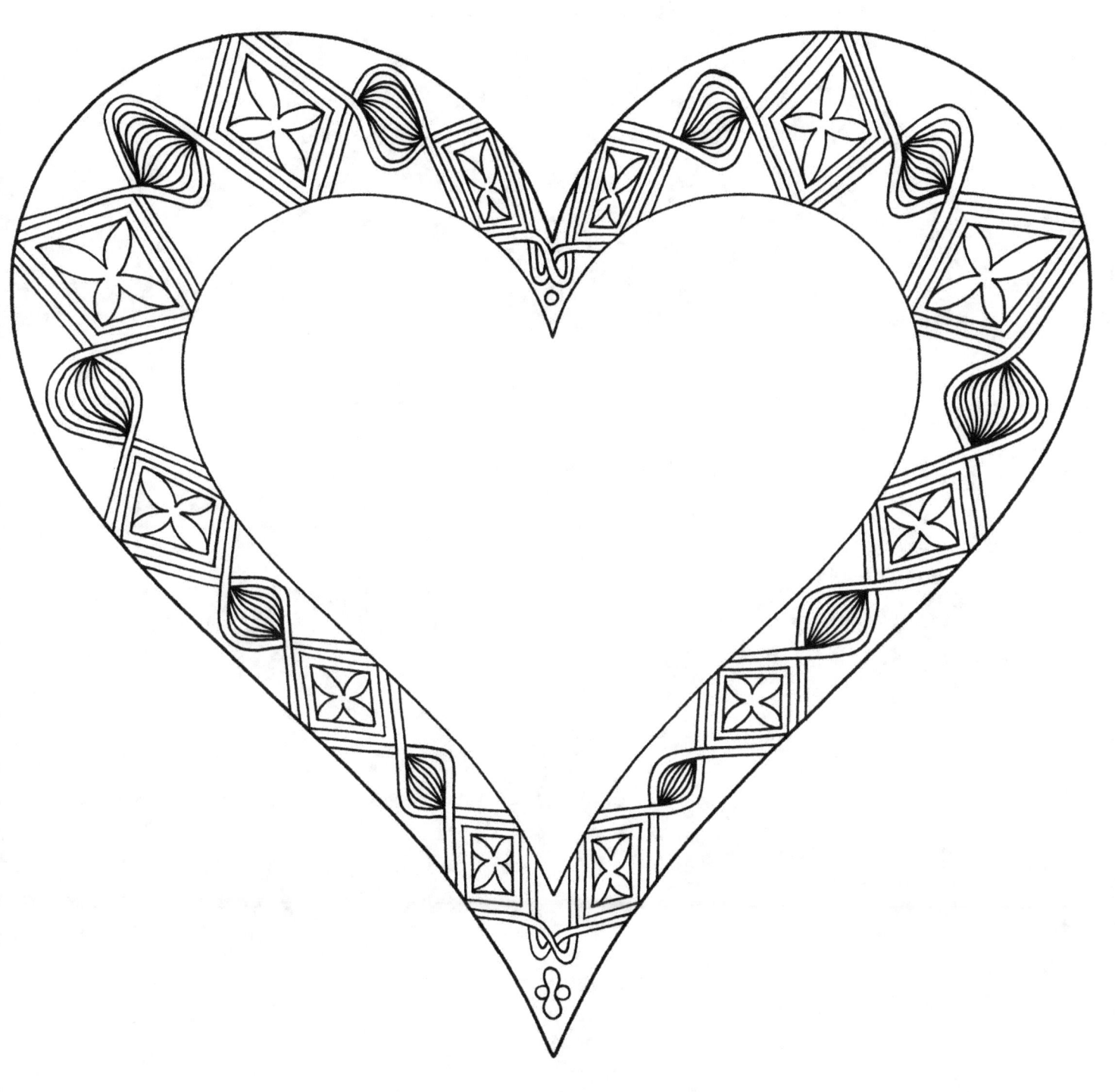

Contributing Artist
Nancy Liu
Taiwan

Facebook : 43Nancy43

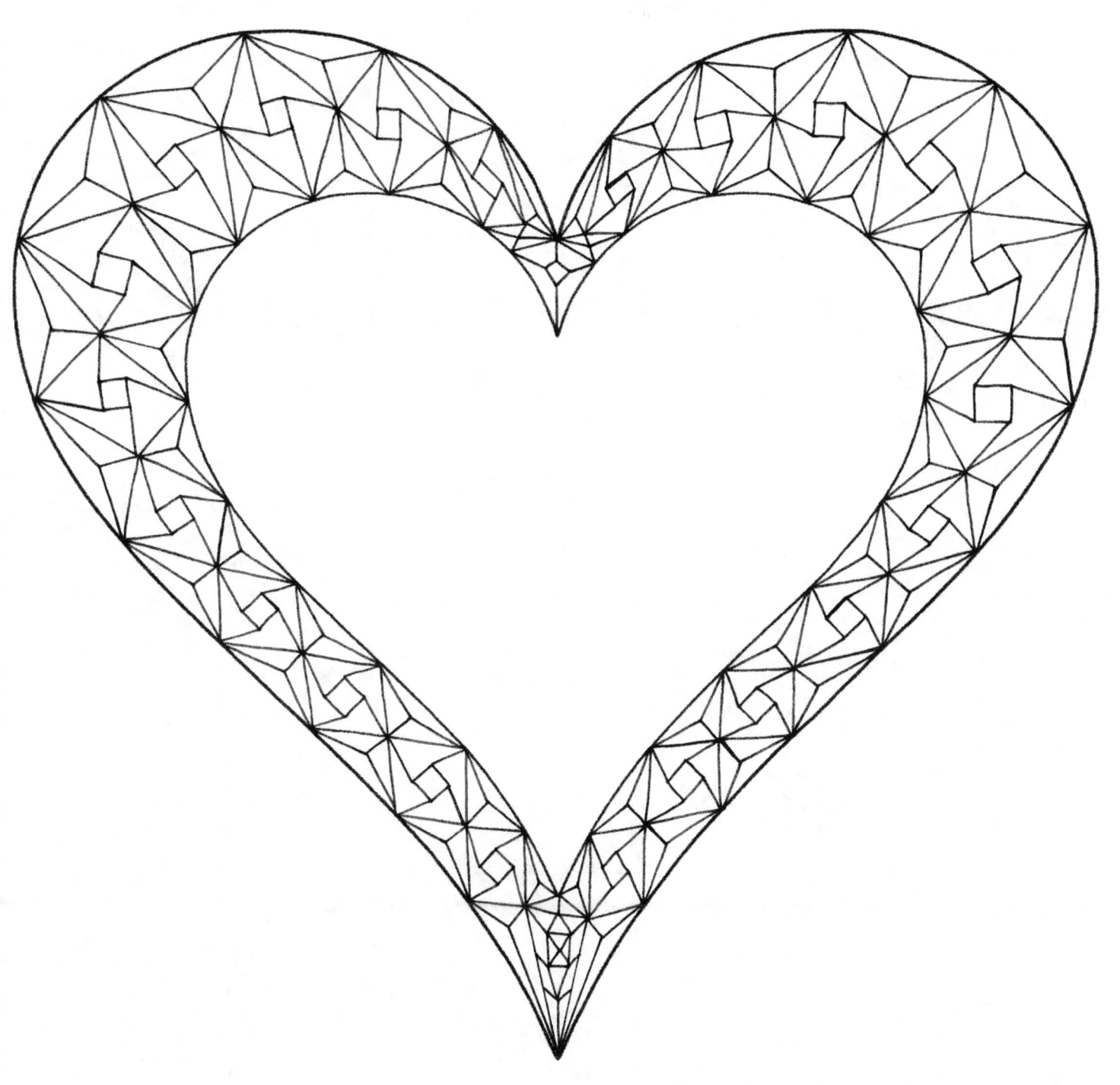

Contributing Artist
Nancy Liu
Taiwan

Facebook : 43Nancy43

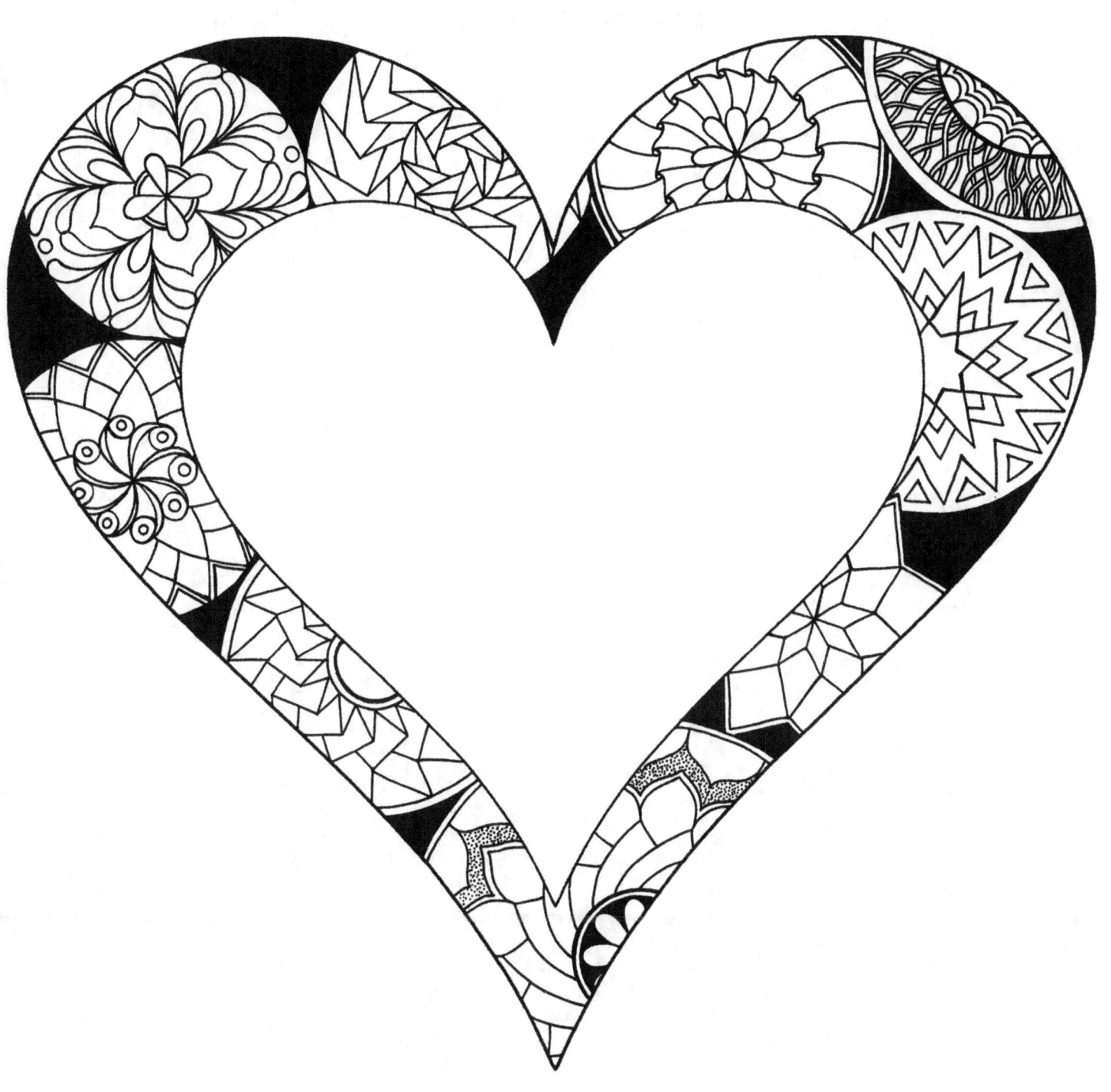

Contributing Artist
Nancy Liu
Taiwan

Facebook : 43Nancy43

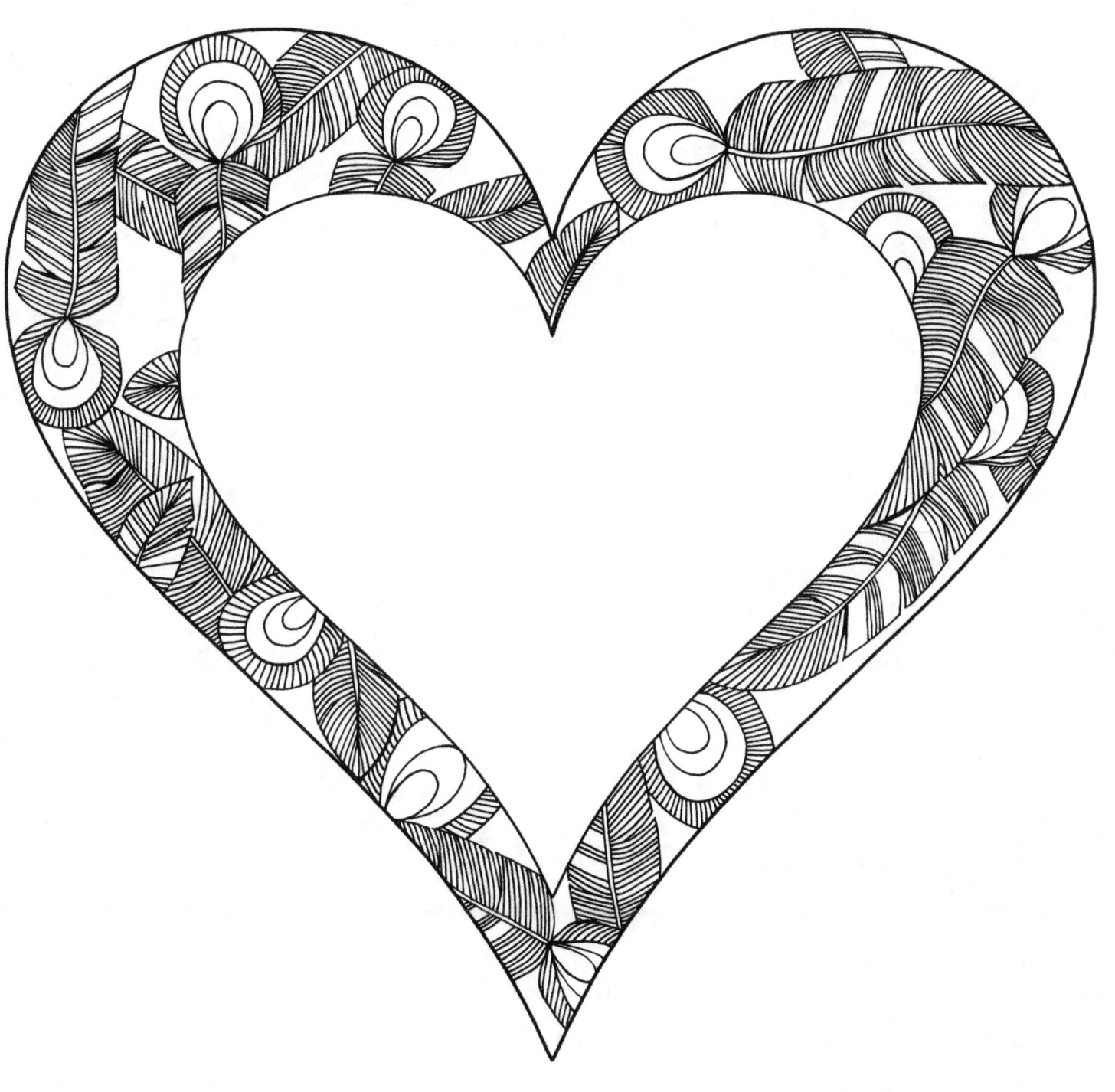

Contributing Artist
Pica Wu
Taiwan

Facebook : picapicadrow2

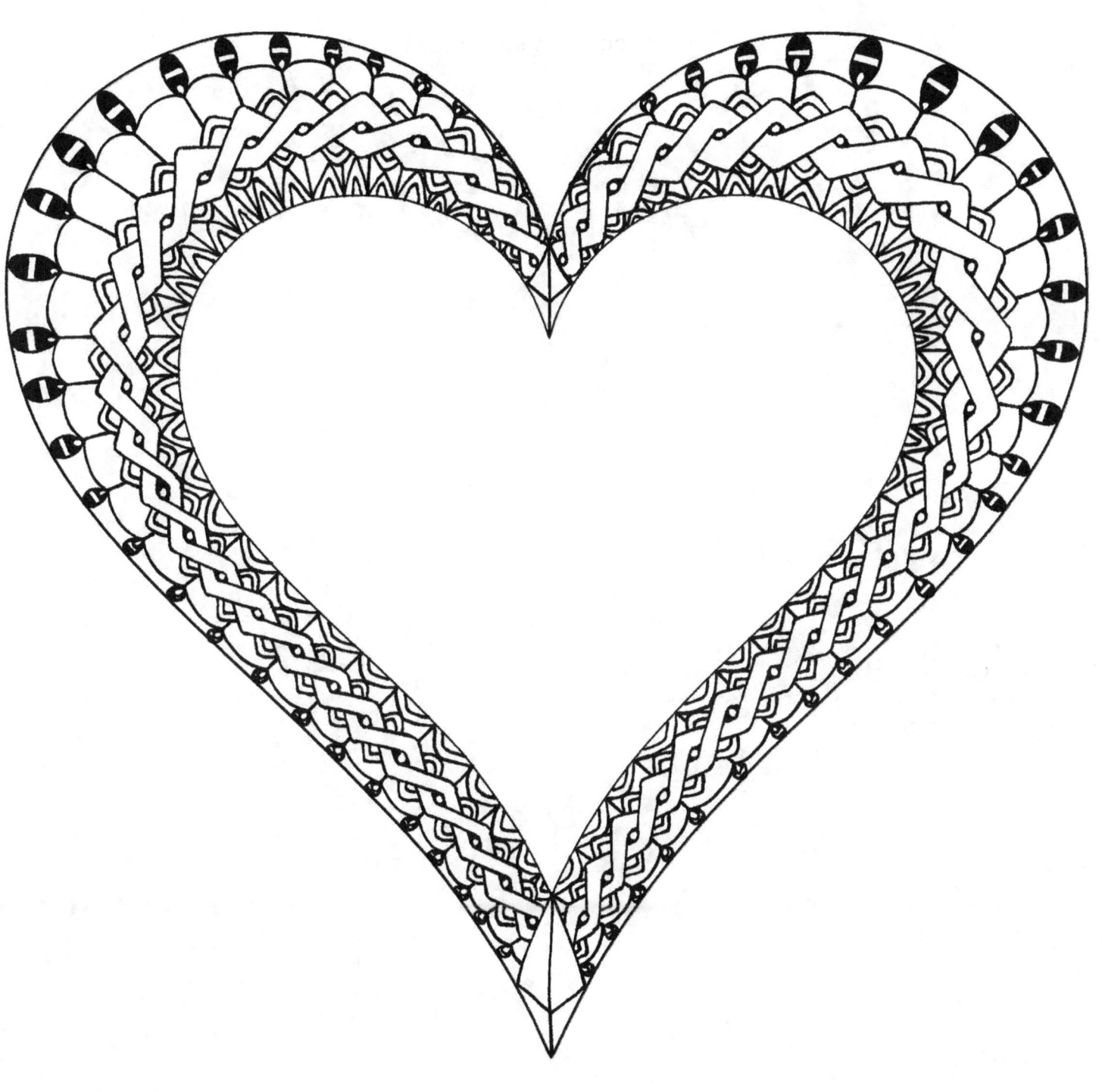

Contributing Artist
Pica Wu
Taiwan

Facebook : picapicadrow2

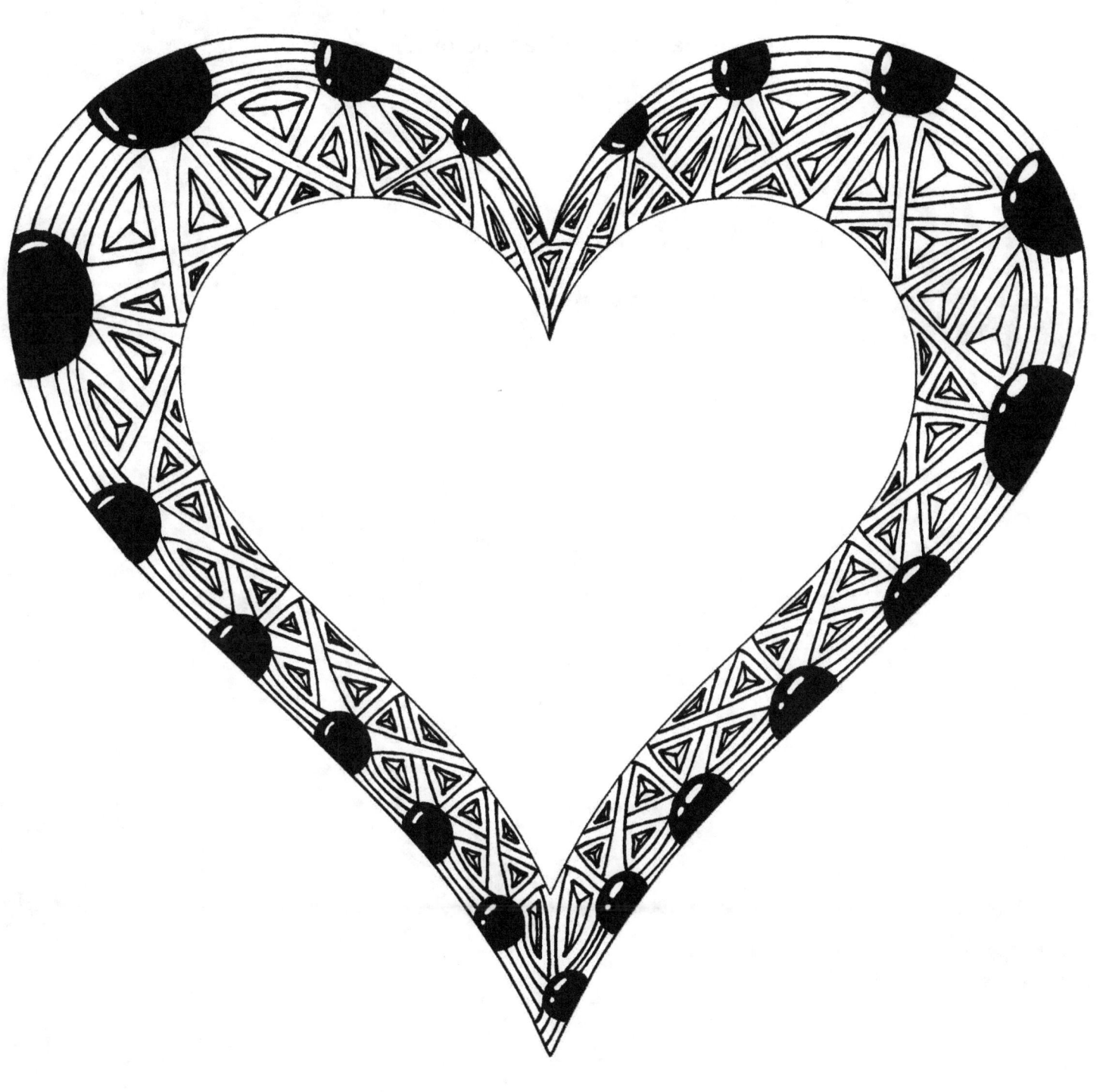

Contributing Artist
Pica Wu
Taiwan

Facebook : picapicadrow2

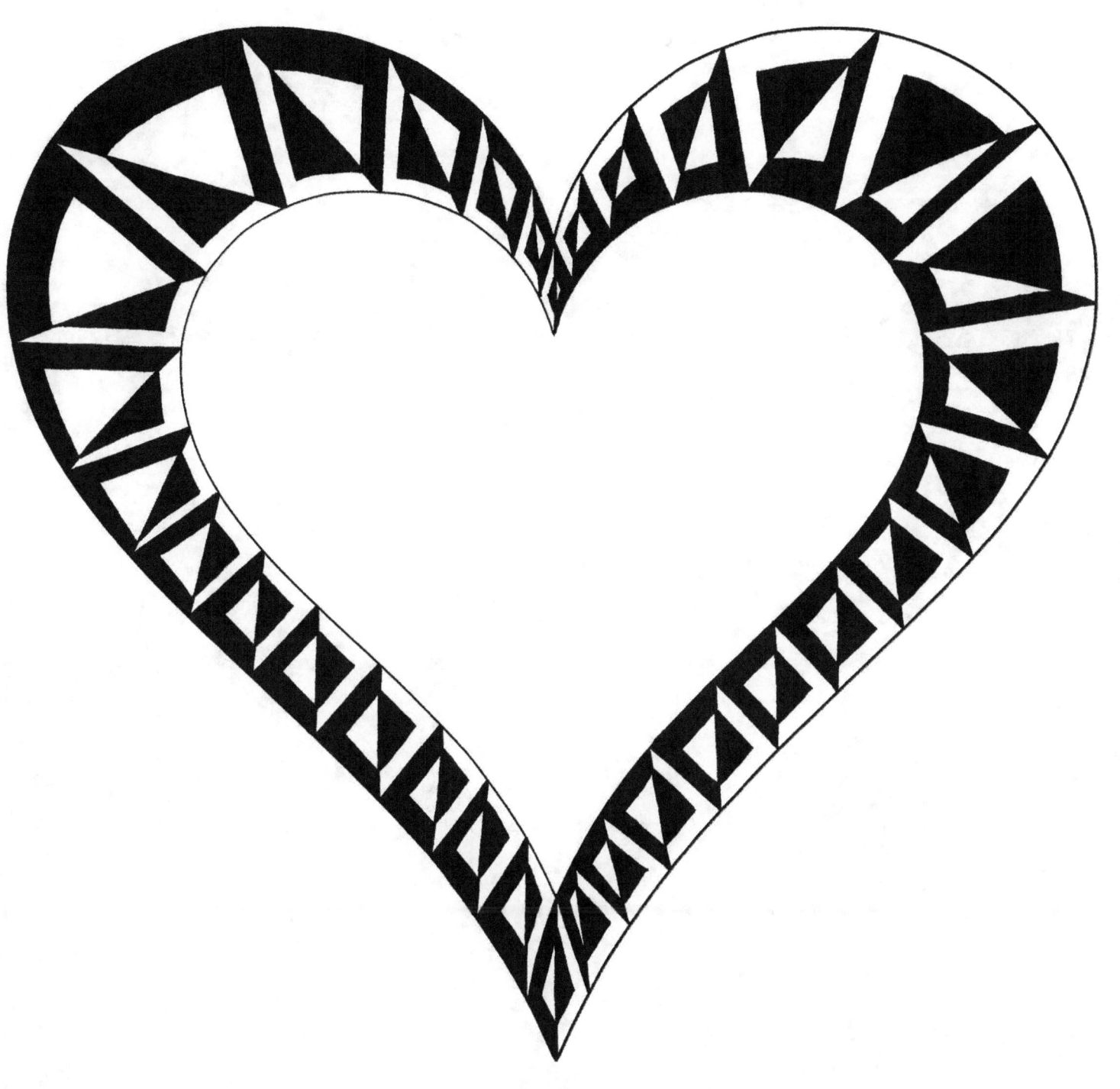

Contributing Artist
Pica Wu
Taiwan

Facebook : picapicadrow2

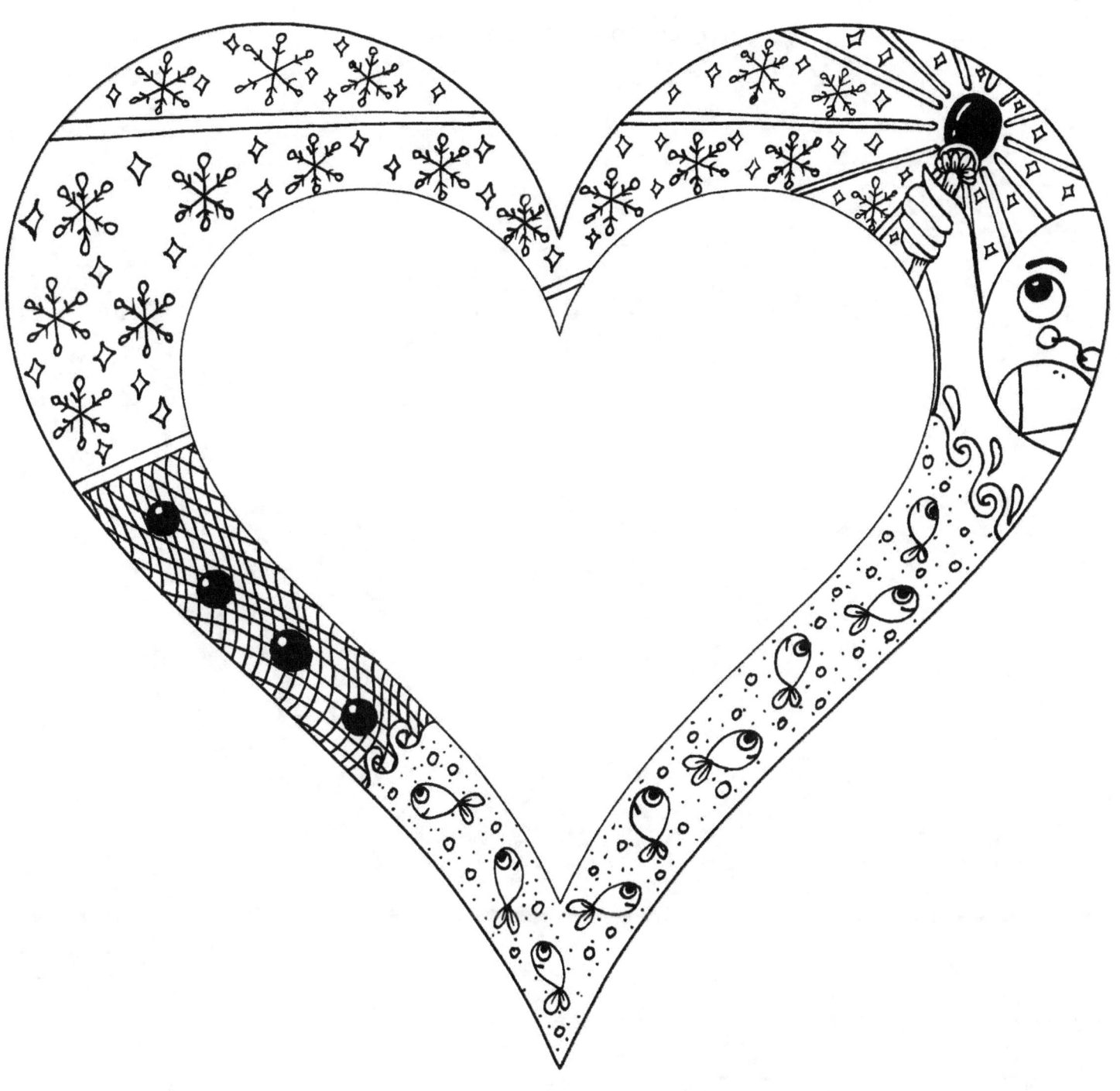

Contributing Artist
Pica Wu
Taiwan

Facebook : picapicadrow2

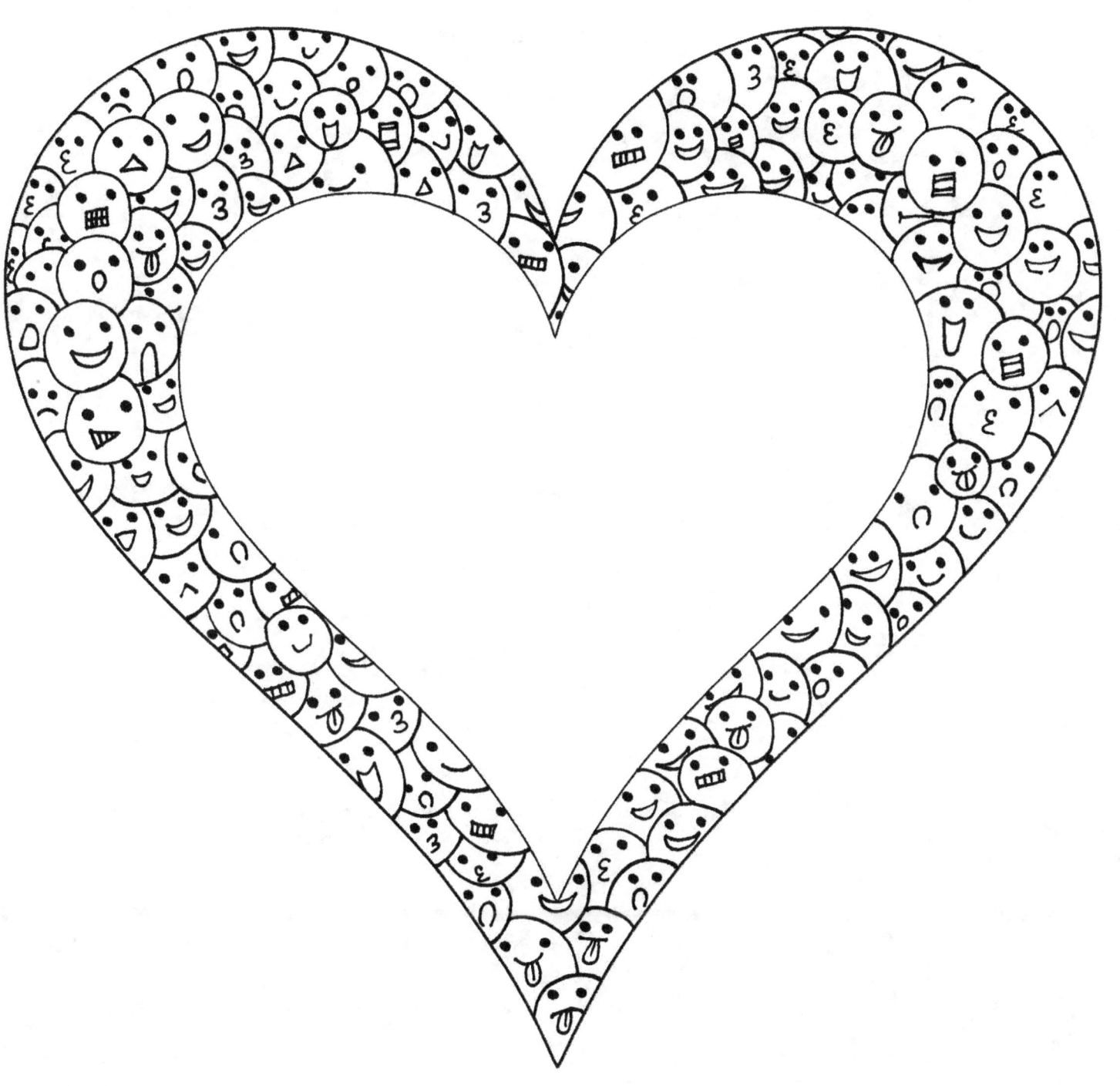

Contributing Artist
Pica Wu
Taiwan

Facebook : picapicadrow2

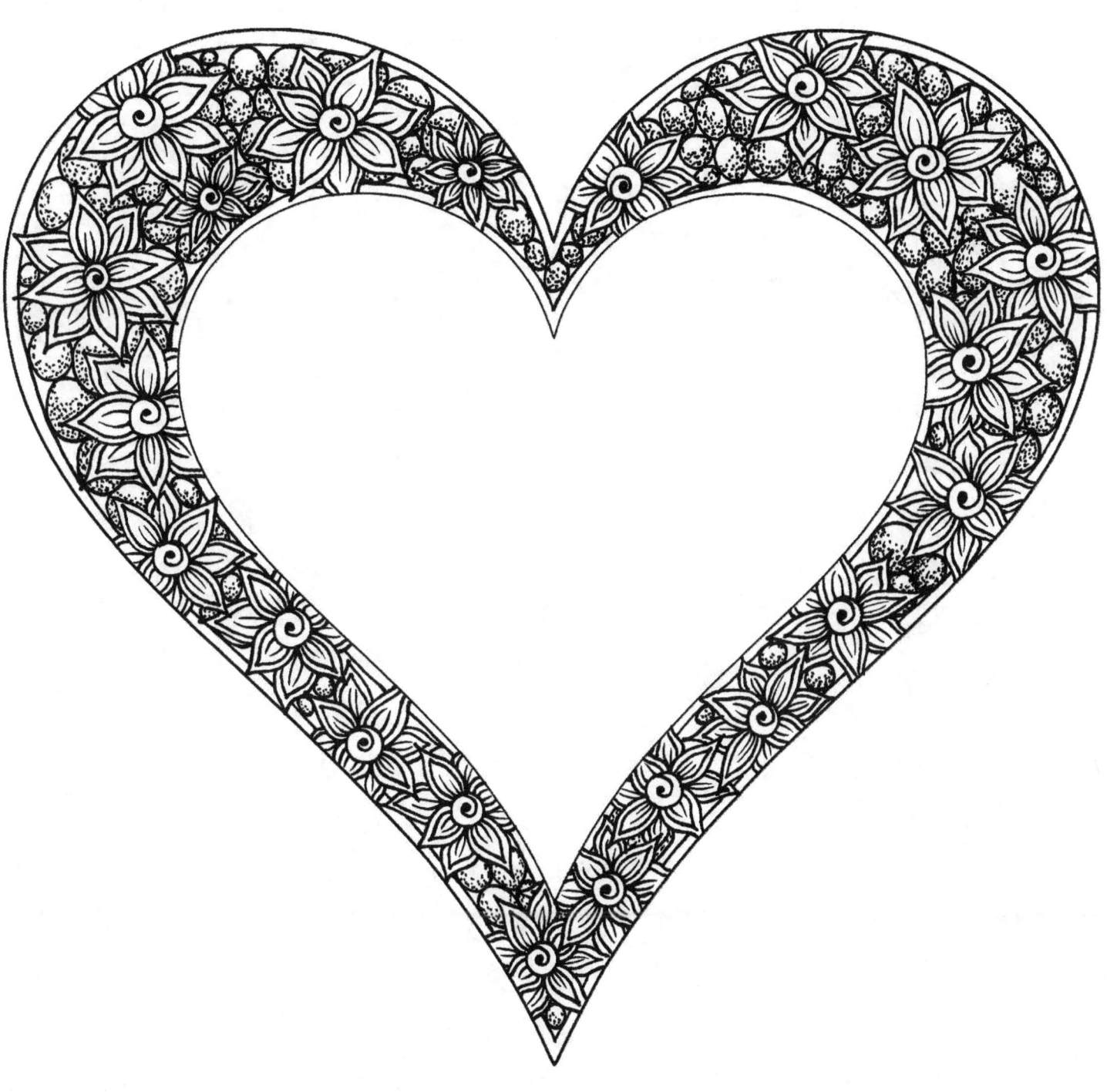

Contributing Artist
Pica Wu
Taiwan

Facebook : picapicadrow2

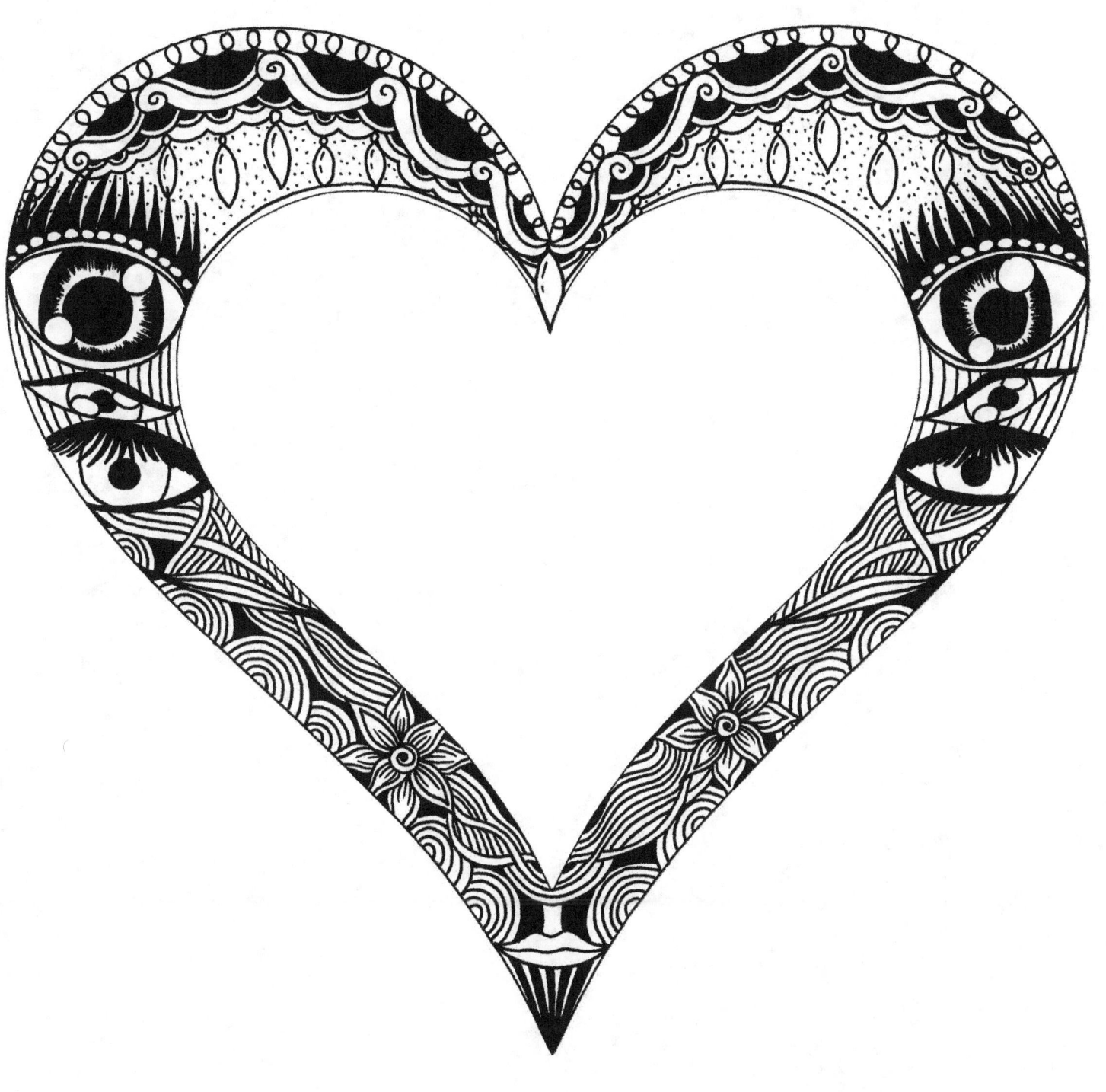

Contributing Artist
Pica Wu
Taiwan

Facebook : picapicadrow2

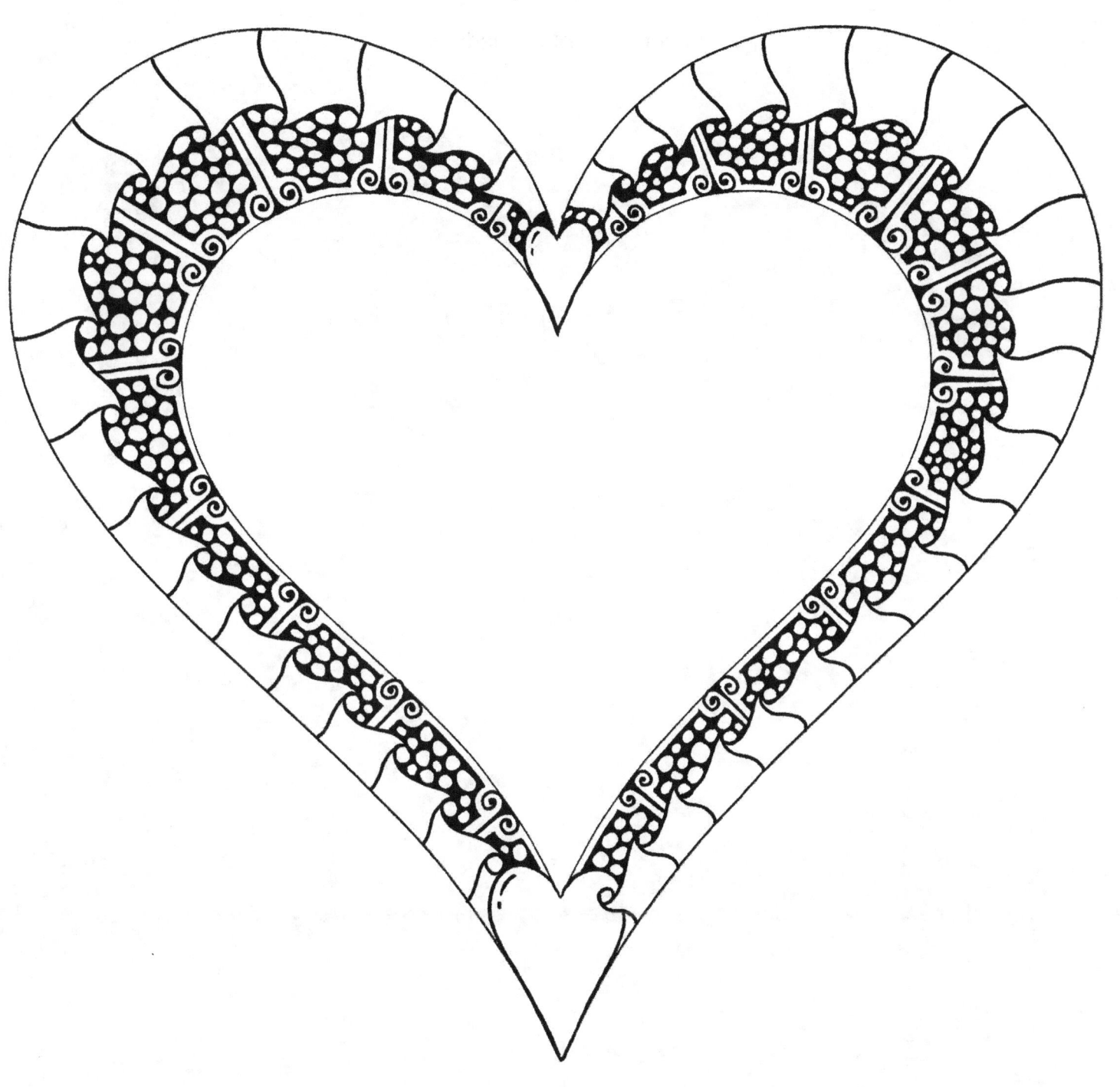

Contributing Artist
Pica Wu
Taiwan

Facebook : picapicadrow2

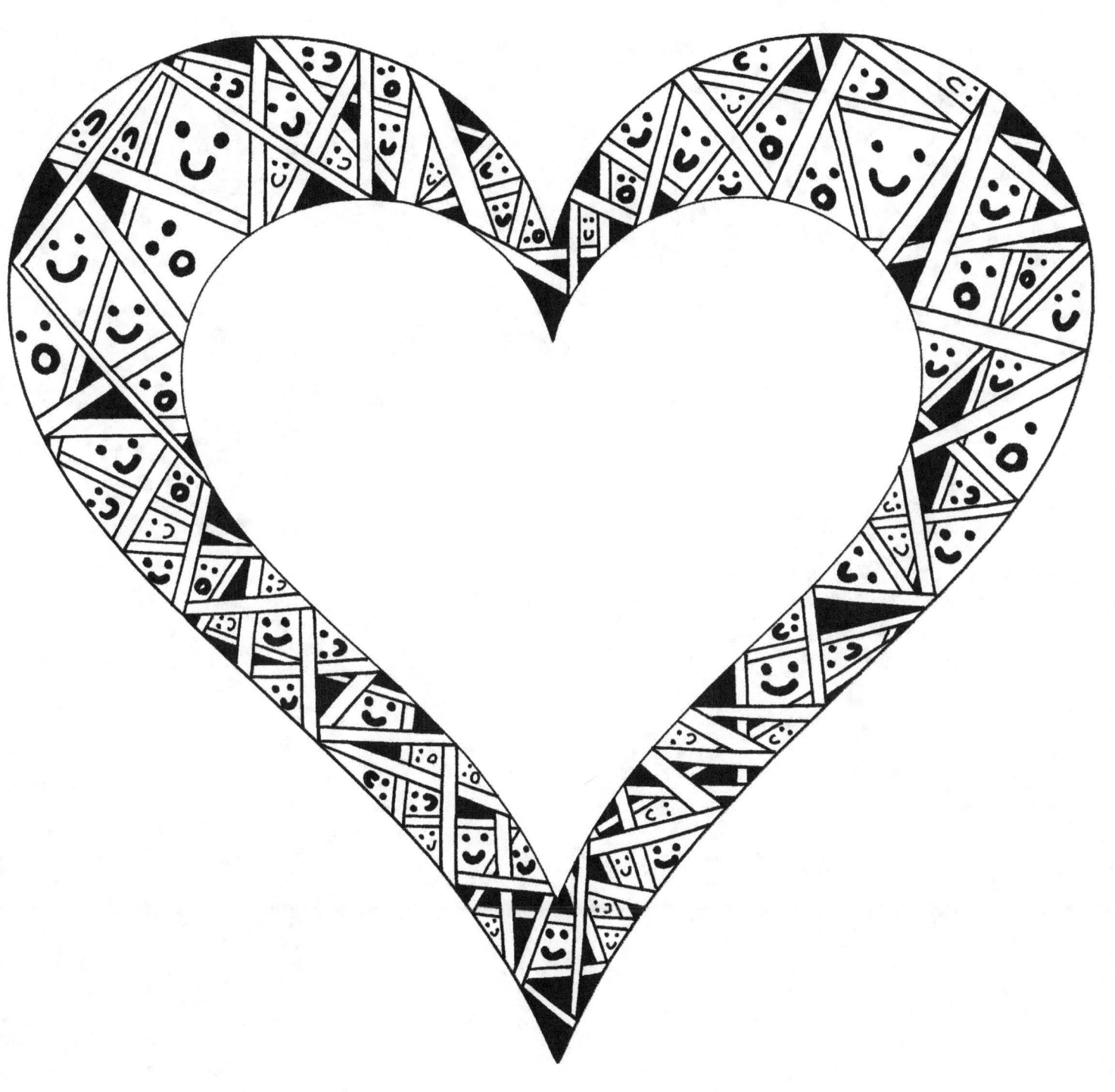

Contributing Artist
Pica Wu
Taiwan

Facebook : picapicadrow2

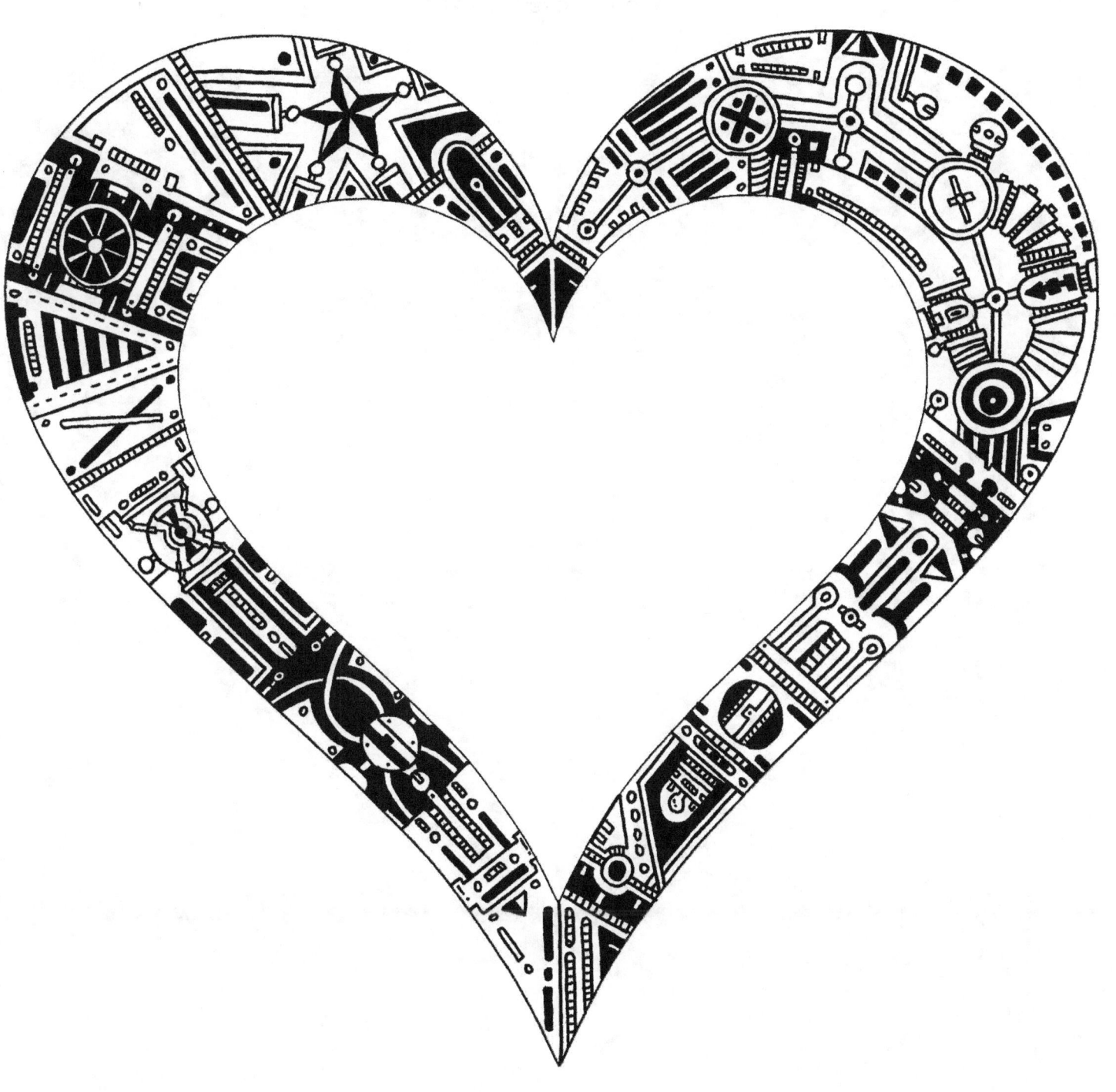

Contributing Artist
Rover Hsiao
Taiwan

Facebook : roverhsiao2015

Contributing Artist
Rover Hsiao
Taiwan

Facebook : roverhsiao2015

Contributing Artist
Rover Hsiao
Taiwan

Facebook : roverhsiao2015

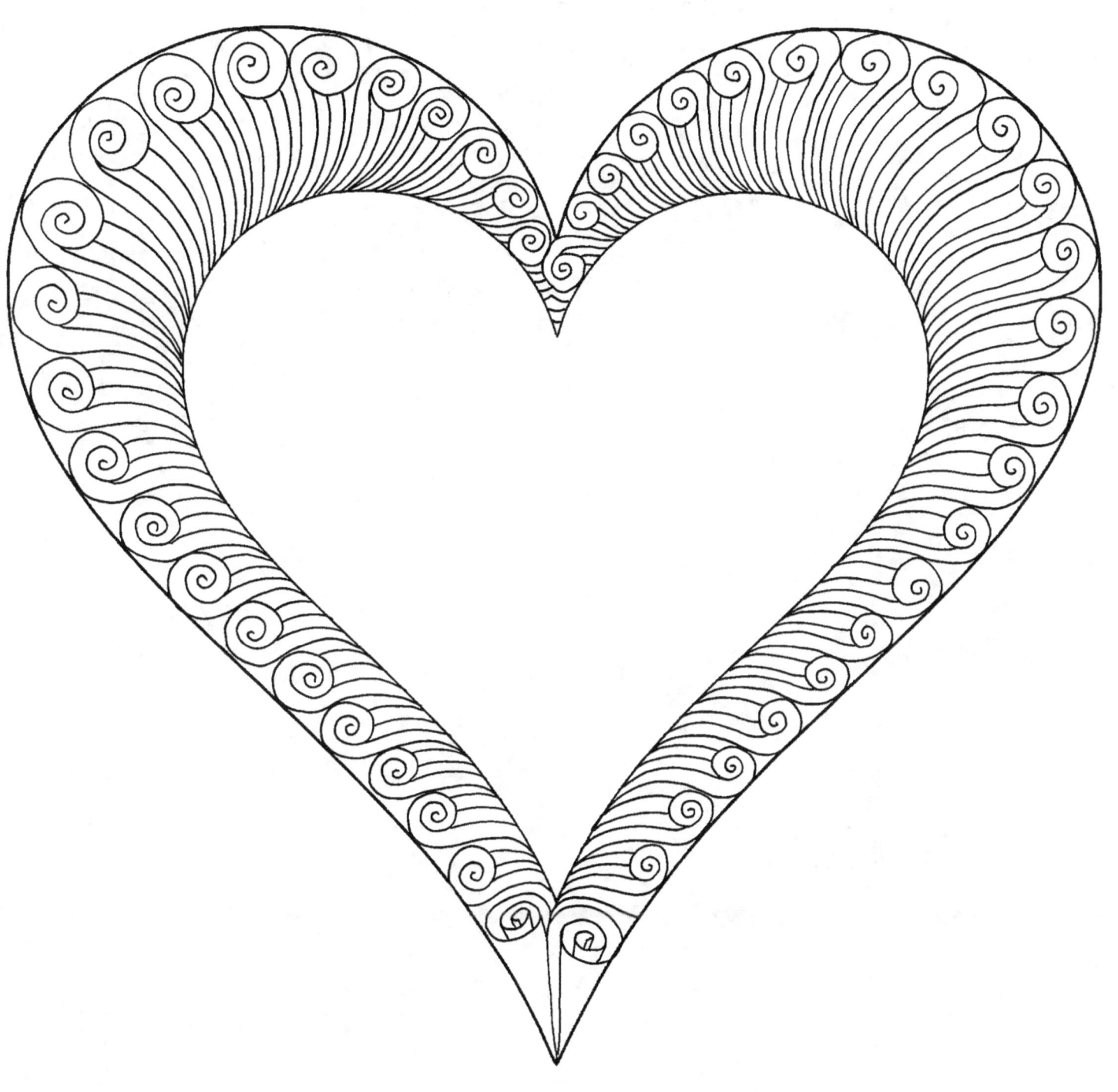

Contributing Artist
Rover Hsiao
Taiwan

Facebook : roverhsiao2015

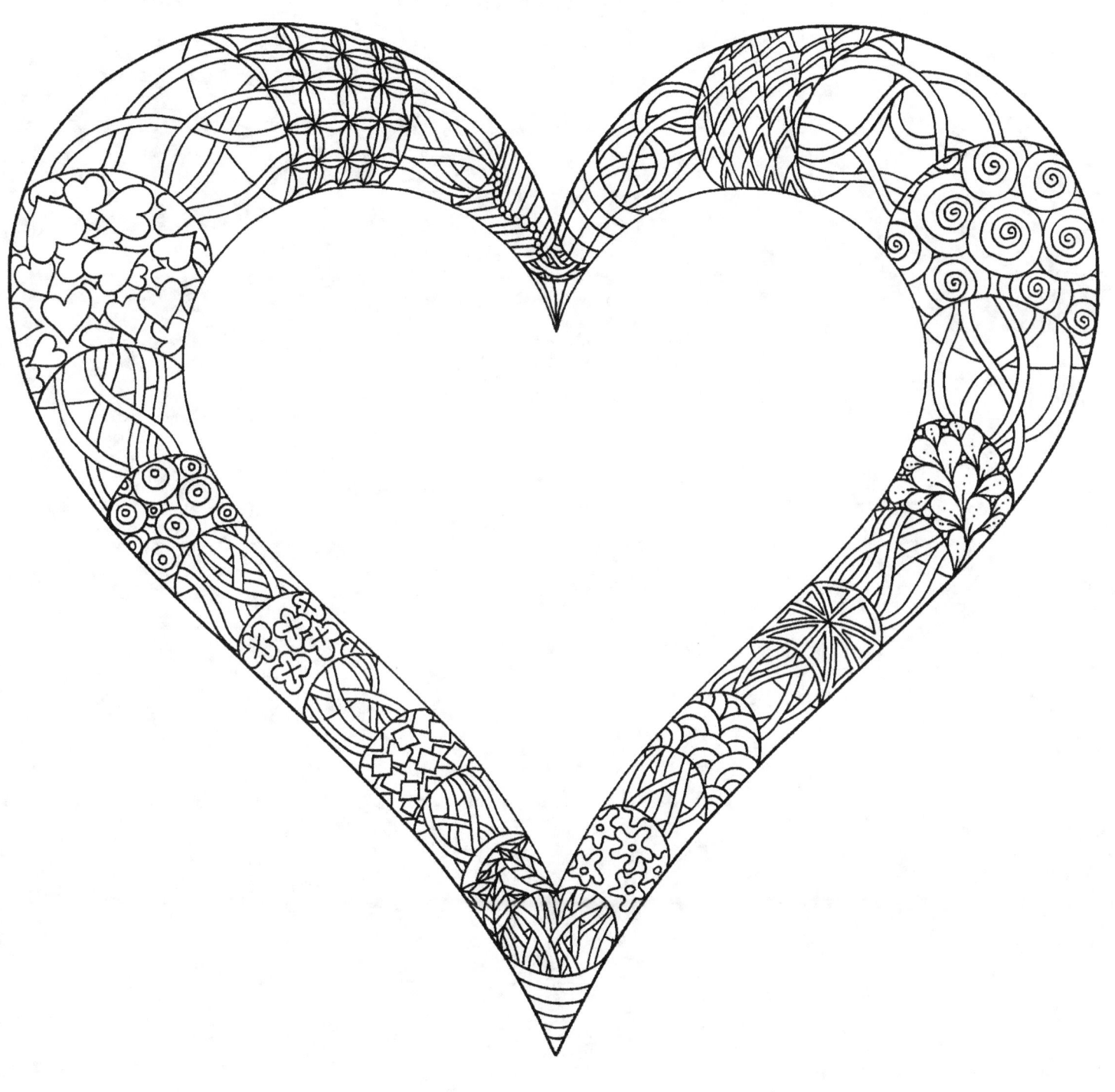

Contributing Artist
Rover Hsiao
Taiwan

Facebook : roverhsiao2015

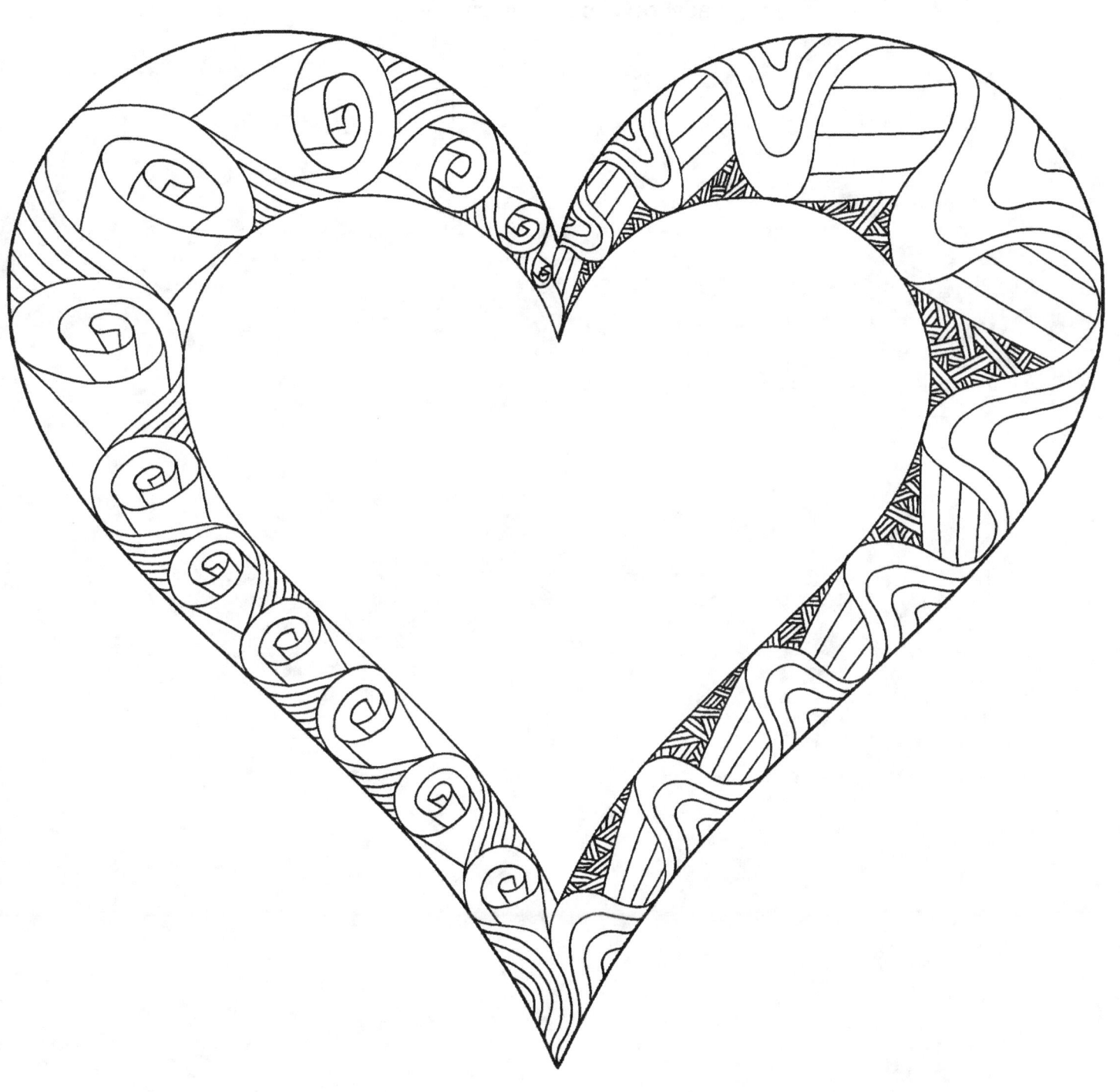

Contributing Artist
Wenyu Lin Small Fish
Taiwan

Facebook : smallfish.smallfish

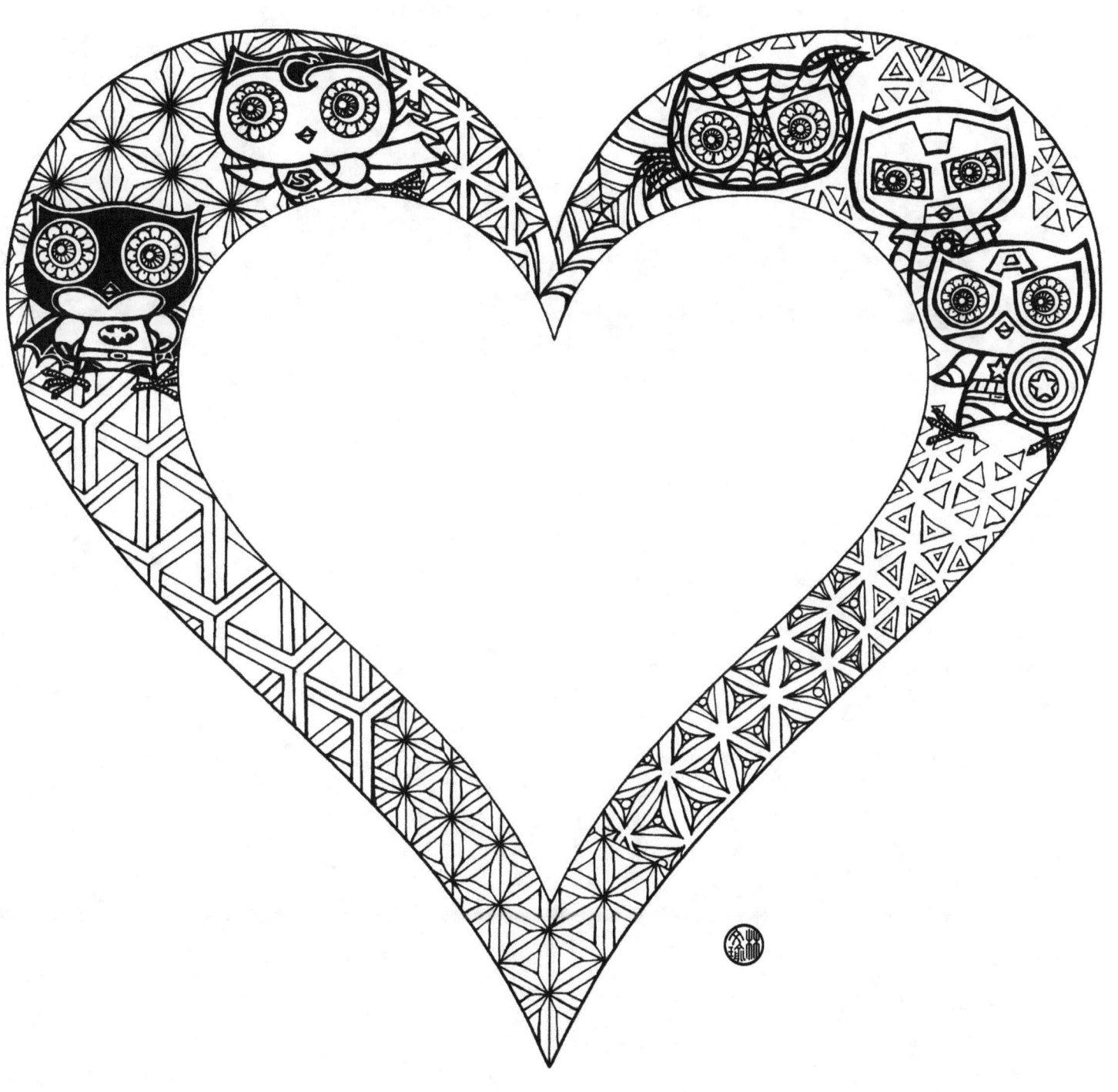

Contributing Artist
Wenyu Lin Small Fish
Taiwan

Facebook : smallfish.smallfish

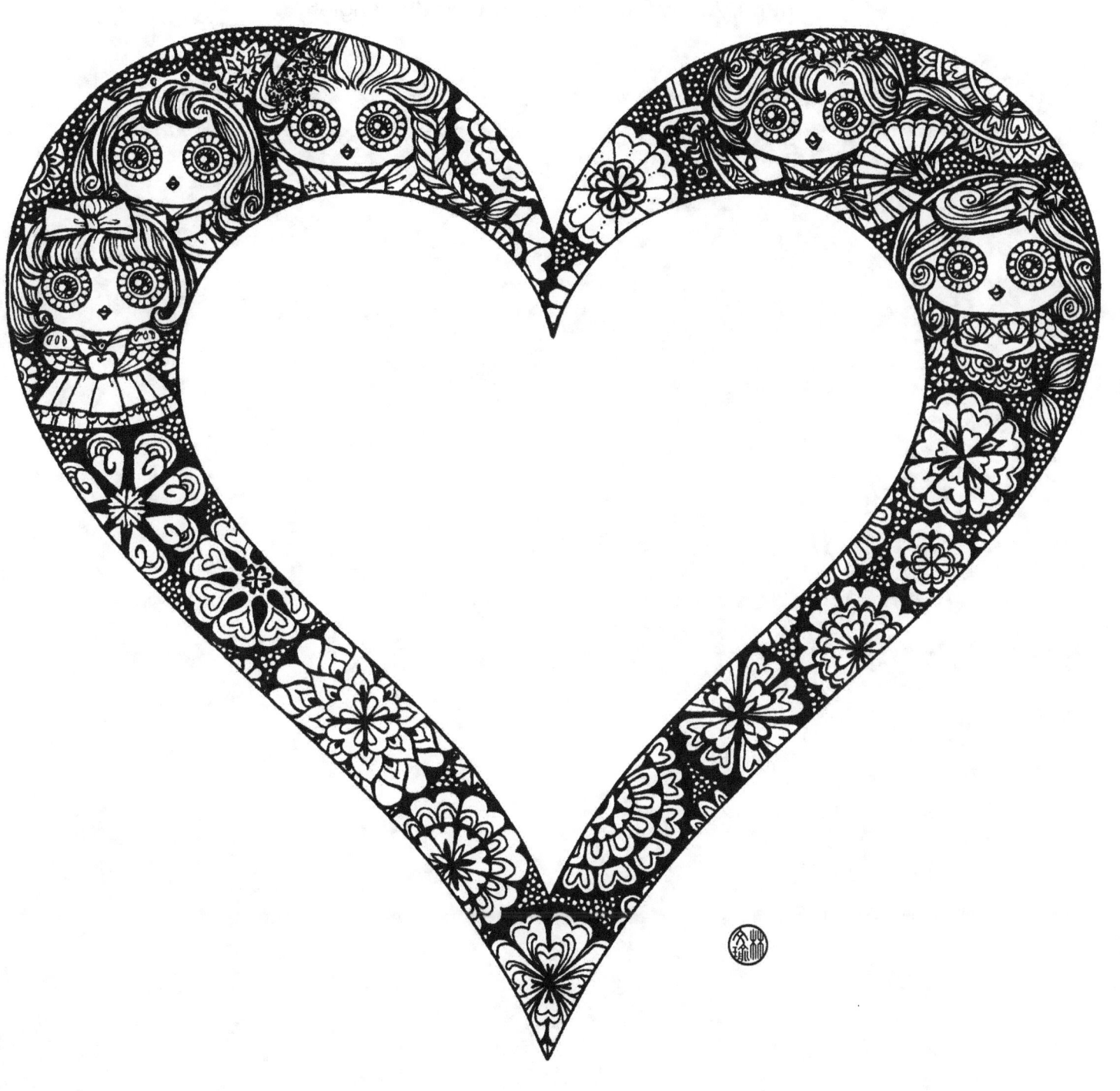

Contributing Artist
Wen Kung
Taiwan

https://www.facebook.com/Wen.Zentangle

Contributing Artist
Wen Kung
Taiwan

https://www.facebook.com/Wen.Zentangle

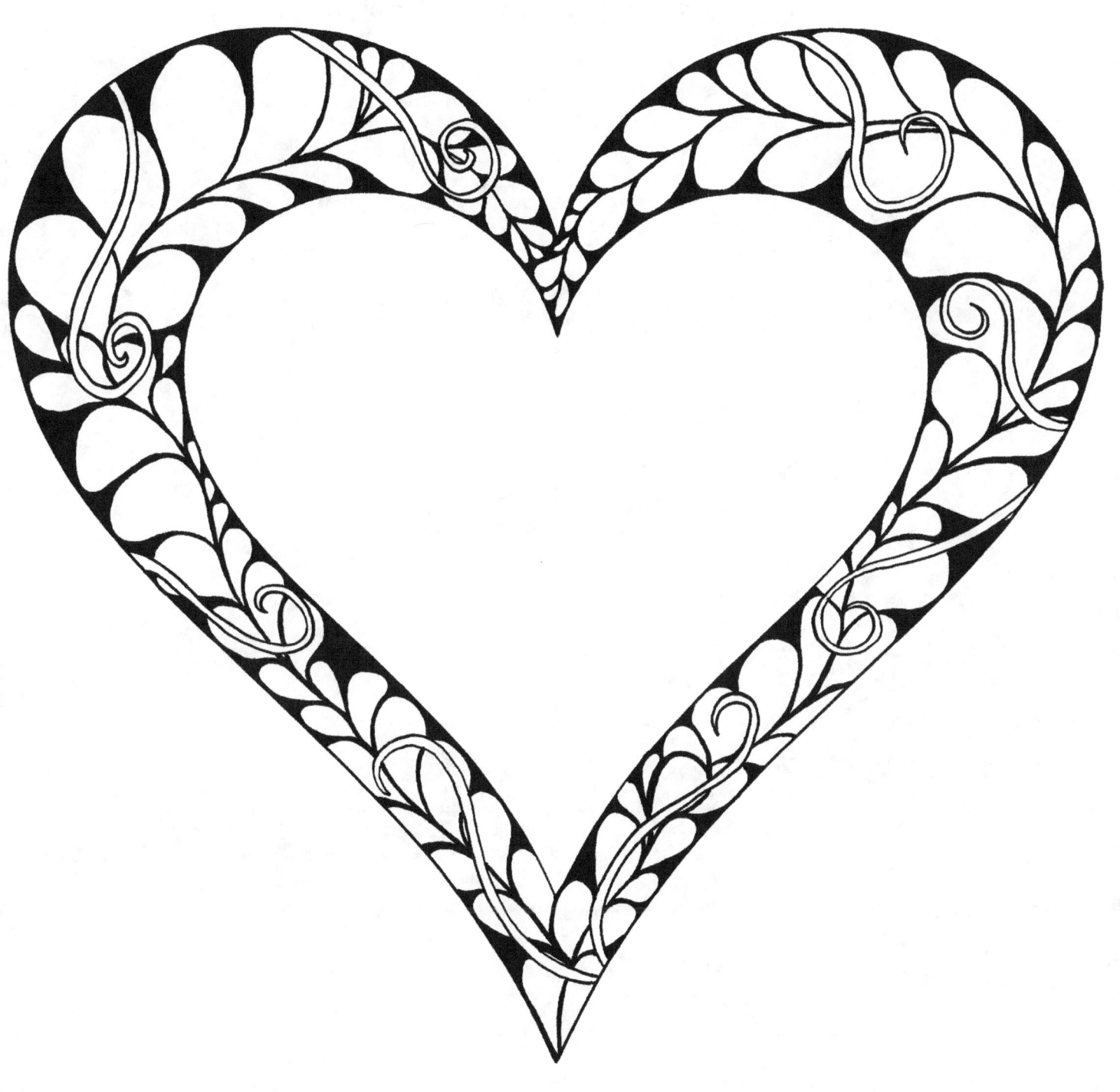

Contributing Artist
Wen Kung
Taiwan

https://www.facebook.com/Wen.Zentangle

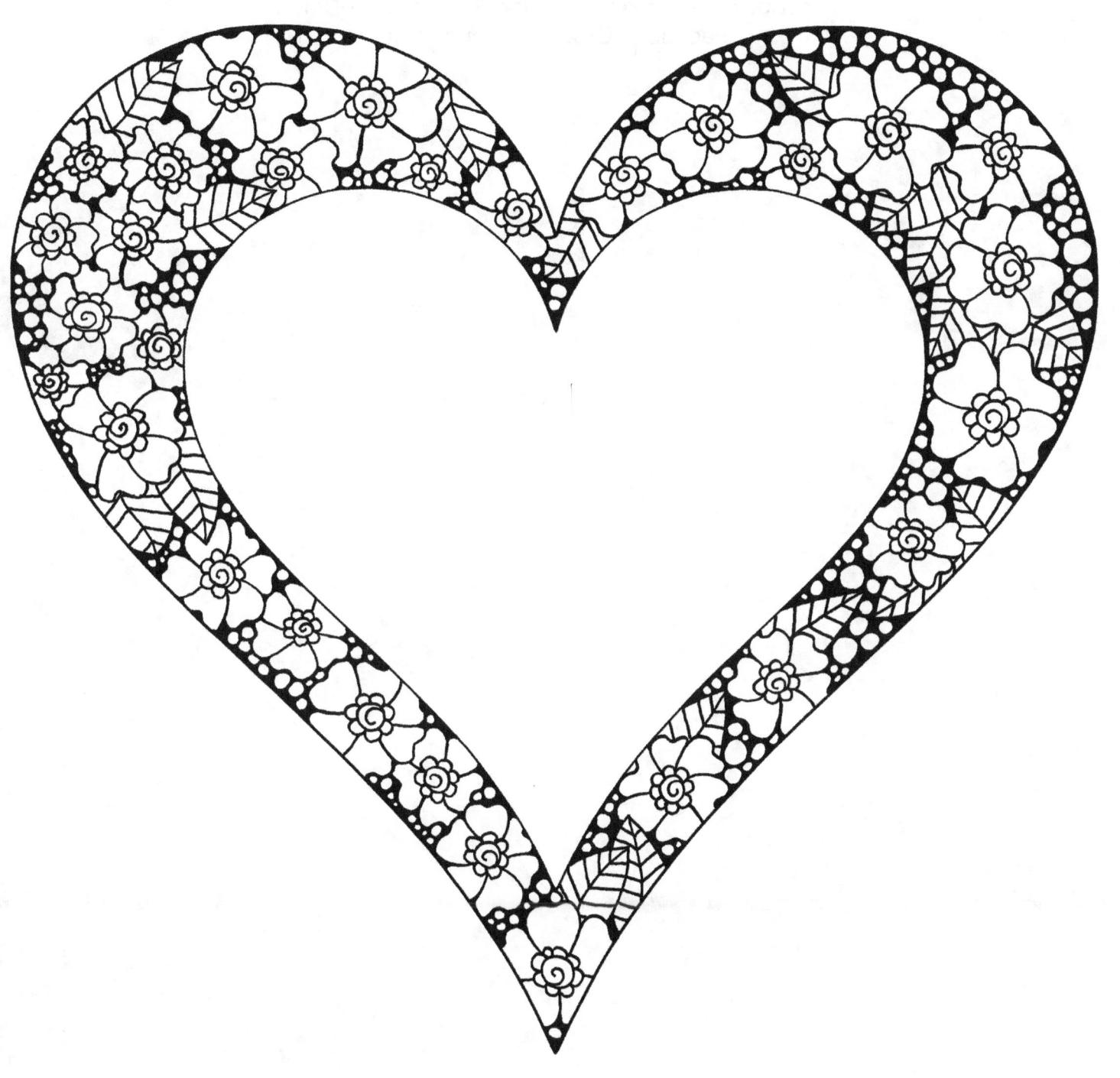

Contributing Artist
DomDomx
France

Facebook : Les-dessins-et-doodles-de-Dom-Domx
Facebook Group : Color.Addict

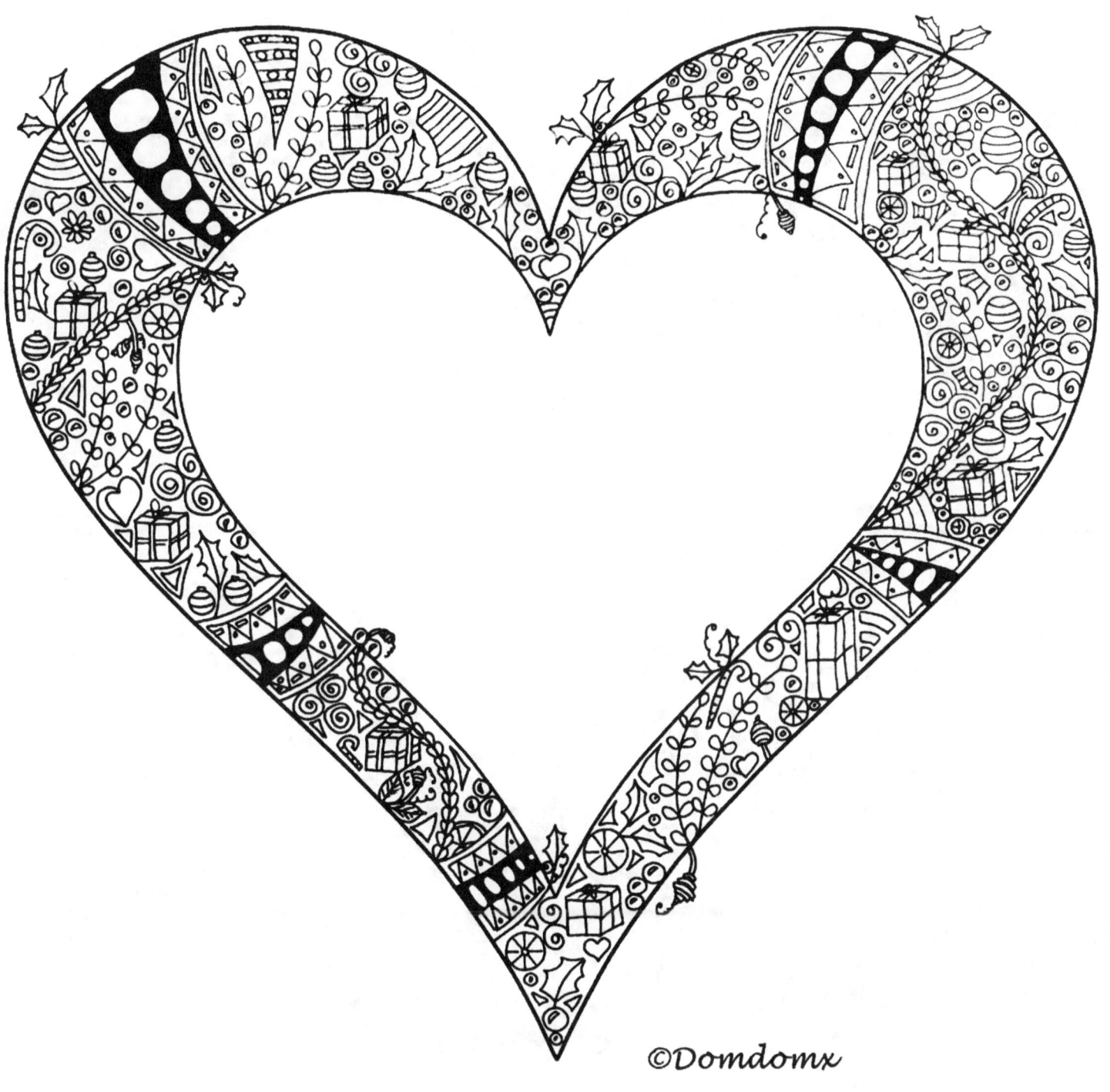

www.ingramcontent.com/pod-product-compliance
Lightning Source LLC
Chambersburg PA
CBHW082325220526
45470CB00008B/2405